MIND MAP
Your Guide to Prosperity and Fulfillment

MIND MAP
Your Guide to Prosperity and Fulfillment

by
Sanford "Buddy" Frumker

Health Associates, Ltd.
P.O. Box 188009
13956 Cedar Road, #146
University Heights, Ohio 44118
(216) 382-3317

ISBN 1-883974-11-9

LCCN 93-79635

Editing, design, typesetting, and printing services provided by About Books, Inc., 425 Cedar Street, Buena Vista, CO 81211, 800-548-1876.

ATTENTION CORPORATIONS, COLLEGES, AND SPIRITUAL ORGANIZATIONS: Quantity discounts are available on bulk purchases of this book for educational purposes or fund raising. Special books or book excerpts can also be created to fit specific needs. For information, please contact Health Associates, Ltd., 13956 Cedar Road #146, P.O. Box 188009, University Heights, Ohio 44118 or call (216) 382-3317.

DEDICATION

To all who experience life as an adventure in self-creation, and thereby universal creation.

Deep Thanks:

To Beatrice, my wife of 46 years, whose total love and sharing were and are a major cornerstone in my self-creation and in my life.

To my children and grandchildren who so infinitely enrich my life.

To Jack and Lois Schwarz, without whom neither the form of this book nor that of my present life could have taken place.

To Linda L. Lewis, whose incredible writing skills and personal interest have been the alchemy and magic that converted my initially academic, scientific, bulky text into this book.

To Doris Palmer, Joan Tillow, and Laurie Regal, who have shared the 38 years of my periodontal practice so as to not only develop a wonderful practice, but for us to mutually develop and enhance each other.

SPECIAL ACKNOWLEDGEMENT:

To my colleague and co-worker Joan M. Hall, whose insights and contributions have been of major importance to me and to the creation of this book. She has transformed the writing into an adventure of self-empowerment and self-creation.

FOREWORD

In 1985, a man with a tremendous background in many different aspects of healing came to the Aletheia Foundation to find the answers to questions that had burdened him for decades. As soon as I started to talk to him, I felt a connection that went beyond the words we were saying to each other. I knew right away he was not going to be a student of mine. Rather he would be an exchanger of wisdom with me and others who had achieved a certain level of consciousness.

This man was Buddy Frumker. His given name is Sanford, but I have always called him Buddy and he prefers the nickname. When he came to Aletheia, he had already conducted workshops around the country on evaluating and correcting malfunctions in the human energy system. He had studied with some of the leaders of energy movement and pattern: Dr. Hazel Parcells, Dr. Richard Broeringmeyer, Dr. Emmanuel Chraskin, Dr. William Donald Kelly, Albert Roy Davis and Walter Rawles. Buddy is a dentist by profession, specializing in treating periodontal disease and head, neck, shoulder and spinal pain. In his dental practice, he went beyond treating the symptoms his patients brought to him. He guided those patients to a higher level of understanding so they became more powerful, integrated human beings.

At Aletheia, Buddy hoped to discover his mission in life. He felt he held a number of pieces to the puzzle of human existence, but lacked a framework for fitting those pieces together. He was so eager for answers and already in such a high state of consciousness that he soon discovered the paradigm for which he had been searching.

This book is one result of Buddy's discoveries. In its pages, he shares the material he studied at Aletheia, but he puts it in a form all his own. Buddy has a great gift for synthesis. He has managed to pull together many of the different techniques we teach at Aletheia into one practical, all-encompassing approach. When I read the manuscript, I recognized many of my statements, and I was delighted by the context into which Buddy fit them.

Buddy used what he learned with us to change his life. Everyone who knows him recognizes the profound effect his internship at Aletheia has had on him. I have watched him become totally involved in the program and, in his own way, use the teachings to expand his life and his consciousness. I tell all those who come to Aletheia to find their own paths to enlightenment, to use what they learn as a general guide only. Each of us is unique and must find the way that is uniquely ours. Buddy not only found his way, but in the process, he also managed to enlarge upon the general guidelines and present them in a form useful to everyone. For that, I thank him.

I thank him, too, for becoming a friend. In our many private conversations, I have found a tremendous source of wisdom within this man. He often reminds me of the great poets for whom he has a natural understanding. He has a way of getting to the heart of things. Always spontaneous in his questions and musings, he shares his knowledge in such a loving manner and with such a lack of ego that he seems unaware of the great influence he has over those around him. I am always pointing out to him his marvelous insights.

You have a great experience ahead of you, dear reader. The words in this book contain the seeds of change. No matter what your current level of consciousness, it will have expanded by the time you reach the last page. And you will have had the privilege of an exchange of wisdom with a powerful and loving mind.

Jack Schwarz
The Aletheia Psycho-Physical Foundation
1068 East Main Street
Ashland, Oregon 97520
(503) 488-0709

HOW TO GET THE MOST OUT OF YOUR EXPERIENCE WITH *MIND MAP*

Since everyone is unique, everyone approaches a book like this in his or her own way. Here are three approaches which can successfully help you extract the most from *Mind Map*.

The preface and first three chapters are introductory. They are also non-interactive, in contrast to the material beginning with Chapter Four, which is totally interactive. From there on you will be doing the exercises and meditations and literally experiencing what they can attain for you.

If you are systematic and scientific, like the author, you will prefer to go through the book exactly as it's written. In this way, you'll get the background material necessary to understand and benefit from the exercises and meditations. This is the first method for using *Mind Map*.

On the other hand, some readers may get impatient going through the introductory material. They are go-getters who want to get right down to doing the core exercises in Chapters Four, Five and Six. Those readers should skim through or skip the introductory material and go right to Chapter Four. They can go back to the introductory material at any time.

Other readers may want to immediately know what this book is about. They want to speedily decide if it's for them. Those people can also skim or skip the introductory material and go right into Chapters Four and Five. When you read and do these meditations and are excited by what they accomplish for you, you then *know* this book is for you. This is the second method of using *Mind Map*.

A third way of employing these techniques is to alternate between the background chapters and the meditation chapters. The important thing is to follow your intuition and use the approach that's best for you.

Whichever way you decide to proceed, be sure to read Chapter Three on breathing for power before you begin the creative meditations of Chapters Seven and Eight. Knowing the proper breathing will greatly increase your effectiveness with these meditations.

Good luck on the wonderful journey that lies before you!

PREFACE: AN INVITATION TO A LIFE OF ABUNDANCE

My goal in this book is to present my understanding of the teachings of Jack Schwarz in step-by-step, workbook form and, thus, give you the means for achieving a life of abundance.

I realize this is an ambitious goal. But I know the Jack Schwarz method leads to abundant, radiant lives. Thousands of people have already learned from Jack how to develop vast personal power and internal resources. Their lives have been dramatically changed. My own life is remarkably different today from the way it was in 1985 when I met Jack.

Jack Schwarz was born in Holland in 1924 and emigrated to the United States in 1957. A year later, he established the Aletheia Psycho-Physical Foundation. Aletheia is the Greek word for truth. Aletheia—a nonprofit center for education and research in all areas of holistics—is located in Ashland, Oregon, and presents year-round workshops by Jack Schwarz.

As a child, Jack realized he had an exceptional ability to control pain and other physiological processes that are thought of as involuntary. He could inflict wounds on himself without feeling pain, then heal those same wounds within seconds. He could control his heart rate and his body's temperature. Jack knew this talent was exceptional only because other people expressed amazement. As he began to investigate the nature of his gift, he learned his abilities were similar to those practiced by holy men in the yogic and Tibetan Buddhist traditions.

A Synthesis of East and West

Wanting to understand and enhance his talent, Jack studied philosophy, history and religion. He found similar ideas in both

Eastern and Western thought. But he found few, if any, Westerners who could do what a highly disciplined yoga or Tibetan monk can. The reason for this, he eventually concluded, was that people in the West devote all their time to the study of ideas and neglect the *practical application* of what they've learned. Consequently, he decided to see whether he could develop a system that would be palatable to the Western mind and include a special emphasis on action and experience. In his synthesis of Eastern and Western thought, Jack developed a system of using one's mind that could be practiced in the context of Western society, and that attained new levels of abundance in all areas of life. You will begin putting this method to work in your own life when you go through Chapter Four of this book.

As he continued his studies, Jack became well-known in research circles for his ability to control his body processes with his mind. His powers were documented at the Menninger Foundation and the Langley Porter Neuropsychiatric Institute. In one instance for Menninger scientists, Jack pushed a six-inch darning needle into the biceps of his left arm. The needle went through skin, muscle and a vein. After pulling the needle out and letting the wound bleed for fifteen seconds, Jack announced he would stop the bleeding. Two seconds later, the blood stopped. Monitoring equipment showed that he was under no unusual stress during this whole exhibition. In fact, all signs indicated he was totally relaxed.

On another occasion, before the Los Angeles County medical and hypnosis associations, Jack picked up burning coals and carried them around in his bare hands for several minutes. When he finally put the coals down, his hand showed no burns or other signs of having been exposed to extreme heat.

The Mind-body Continuum

Jack believes there is an enormous power surrounding all of us. He calls this power the universal mind and describes it as a large field of energy and information that fills the universe. This universal mind is the intelligence that created the universe and keeps it functioning. The human mind is part of the universal mind. When we use our human minds to gain access to it, we can turn universal power into personal power. We can achieve almost anything with this newly acquired ability. We can, as Jack does, control our own physiology—and much more.

Jack feels that part of his mission in this life is to teach others how to achieve the personal power he has achieved. He has developed a program at Aletheia designed to empower others. He also travels throughout the world demonstrating his abilities and sharing his methods for achieving the miraculous.

A Direct Message

On a friend's recommendation, I bought Jack's first book, *The Path of Action*. I was astounded and thrilled. This work seemed to be a practical application of the insights of the poet William Blake, who had been my idol for a long time. Jack's book seemed to be speaking directly to me, touching on all I had encountered in my lifetime search for the meaning of life. I was sixty years old and had investigated just about every discipline that promised an answer to the question: *What is the purpose of life?* I had yet to find one that could account for life in a way that made sense to me.

Any program that purported to offer insight into life's meaning had to have a basis in science for me to accept it. I had a scientific background. I had built a successful dental practice, specializing in periodontics, bite problems, and head, neck and shoulder pain. I had pioneered many of the treatment techniques in these areas and had written a book and numerous articles in the field. I could not accept any system that substituted superstition for science. I was looking for a powerful synthesis.

The Path of Action offered that synthesis. What Jack described in that book was a search similar to my own and a hunger for meaning that matched mine. After reading it I had to meet Jack Schwarz. I flew to Oregon and took a three-day course called "Personal Health Training."

An Answer to a Life-long Riddle

The first thing Jack did in the workshop was look at my aura. Without me saying a word he then spent forty-five minutes telling me all about my life and health. He was right in everything he said. He told me I had prostate trouble and some problems with my sinuses and digestive tract. He told me where I had come from and what I had been doing for the past sixty years. And then he told me the purpose of my life: "You will be a master map maker."

At the time I was not sure what he meant. But I was awed with all he knew about me, just from reading my aura. I decided to ask him to interpret some very important lines of poetry for me. The lines were from Oscar Wilde's "The Ballad of Reading Gaol."

> *Yet each man kills the thing he loves . . .*
> *The coward does it with a kiss,*
> *The brave man does it with a sword!*

I first encountered those lines when I was in junior high school. I was puzzled by their meaning. At the time, something told me if I could ever find anyone to interpret those lines to my satisfaction, I should spend my life studying with that person. Consequently, I asked every teacher I ever had—all the way through high school, college and graduate school—for an explanation. I heard nothing that made sense to me. These three lines of poetry remained the riddle of my life.

When I asked Jack why each man kills the thing he loves, Jack answered immediately. It was obvious, he said. Then he explained that whatever happens to us in life, good or bad, we become attached to it. If we have problems, solving them becomes our focus. We make our problems such a large part of our lives that we have, in effect, fallen in love with them. The same thing happens with our successes. We become so enamored of what we achieve that we want to bask in its glory forever.

These kinds of attachments, he said—whether to problems, successes or both—take us away from our purpose in life, which is to continually move to higher levels of consciousness and awareness. To evolve, we must use our problems and successes as stepping stones instead of becoming so attached to them that we cannot move on. This does not mean we can't pay attention to our problems or glory in our achievements; it means once we have removed an obstacle or enjoyed a success, we cut ourselves free of any attachment and integrate what we have learned into a more powerful self.

To do this requires tremendous courage. Change is what people fear most. Cowards kiss their problems and achievements and remain attached to them, thereby killing the opportunity for growth. Brave individuals cut their attachments so they can move to a higher level of consciousness.

When Jack finished his explanation of the riddle from Oscar Wilde, I knew I had found my teacher. This was the first interpretation that made sense to me. Examples from my own life backed up what he said. I thought, for instance, of my contemporaries who had achieved success in a small area of life, as I had in dentistry—and then become so enamored of that success, so attached to it, that they failed to experience the huge world around them.

"Renounce and Enjoy"

I was ready to study with Jack, to learn how to practice the kind of non-attachment he was talking about. I had read extensively about this non-attachment. In particular, I remembered a story about Mahatma Gandhi, who was asked by a young reporter to explain in twenty-five words or less the reason he had led such a successful life, one so full of great achievement. Gandhi answered, "Young man, I can indeed tell you what I did to achieve my great successes. But I do not need as many as twenty-five words. I need only three. And those three words are *Renounce And Enjoy*."

After meeting Jack, I felt I had the opportunity to put Gandhi's simple yet profound philosophy into action. I was ready to learn Jack's way of non-attachment. I sensed that by cutting my present attachments, I would not forget or leave them. Rather, I would augment them. By becoming non-attached, by being free to change and grow, I could add more and greater loves to my life. I could achieve higher levels of consciousness and a life of abundance and bliss.

Restoration of Physical Health

At the Personal Health Workshop, without any hint from me, Jack told me I had a prostate problem. He was correct. I had a major problem. My urologist told me my grossly enlarged prostate gland was threatening my life. Because I could never completely empty my bladder, I was toxic. The urologist urged me to have surgery immediately.

I put him off. I felt surgery would solve the immediate problem but would do nothing to correct the conditions causing it. I'd studied enough to know that if I could get my own body to correct the problem, I would have gotten to the root cause. I would also have increased my body's ability to keep itself healthy. I thought Jack might help.

Jack never diagnosed, treated or discussed my prostate problem. Instead, he evaluated me and discovered problems with my metabolism. He found that my body was not metabolizing certain elements that it needed. This breakdown of my metabolic functioning was affecting not only my prostate and entire system, but also my adrenal glands, thymus, liver and pancreas. My brain wasn't operating at full power either.

The program I worked out (yes, *I* worked it out—with Jack's guidance) dealt with all of me. I learned about how my body was functioning and how each part of me related to every other part. After three months of working at this program, my prostate problems had lessened dramatically. In four months, they were nearly gone.

My urologist was amazed when he examined me and found that the gland was now only slightly enlarged. I was no longer a candidate for surgery. In fact, my whole body was healthier than it had been in a long time.

I had experienced for myself what I somehow always knew. My own body has all the knowledge and tools it needs to restore health and remain healthy. Healing does not come from outside the body; it's an inside job. By learning how to listen to my body, I found it could heal itself.

Boost to Financial Health

Through the Aletheia Institute, Jack offers a four-year internship program emphasizing human energy systems and self-regulation. I enrolled in this internship and am now completing my sixth year. As I began my formal internship, I was achieving not only physical health, but total health—mental, emotional and spiritual. My financial health, however, was put in great danger by the program. To be an intern required my traveling across the country to Oregon at least ten times a year for courses. Such trips were expensive; there was airfare, tuition, car rental, motel and food costs. At first, I didn't see how I could possibly find the time or the finances to make such journeys. If I cut down my dental practice, I would have the time, but then I wouldn't have the money. It seemed an impossible dilemma, a Catch-22 situation.

However, I knew the time had come for me to move my life into new areas. As much as I love dentistry, I could not achieve my expanded life in that practice alone. I knew I had to give up my full time attachment to my work. Releasing that attachment would afford me the time I needed to move on.

During the start of my internship, I began to discover how to use the power of my total mind to transcend and go beyond my problems, exactly as you will learn in Chapters Four, Five and Six. I learned that when we empower our mind and turn our problems over to it, we will overcome them.

So following my learnings at the Aletheia program, I empowered my mind. Then using mainly the meditations in Chapter Five, I turned the problems over to my total mind. It set up an investment program that brought me all I needed—both in time and finances—to continue with the Aletheia program. Thanks to learning to use my total mind, in the next five years I made more money than in my whole previous life.

Framework for Everyone

Remarkable as his own powers are, Jack's greatest gift is his ability to help others empower themselves. Very few people who posess unusual abilities understand the mechanics of how to *teach* these abilities. Not only does Jack understand how he achieved his abilities, but he also has the insight to guide others to greatly enlarge their powers.

Soon after I began applying Jack's teachings, I discovered I could make life what I wanted it to be!

I was not alone in this remarkable awakening. Hundreds of people have gone through the Aletheia program. Some had been told they suffered from incurable health problems when they began to work with Jack. Some were burdened with seemingly unsolvable emotional problems. Jack did not attempt to cure or treat these people or to hand them solutions. Instead, he taught us all how to empower ourselves, and then tap the more powerful resources we had created within ourselves.

The results were breathtaking. We all literally became new people—more powerful and resourceful people. Chronic health problems disappeared. Allergies vanished. One woman with a degenerative condition got out of her wheelchair and went back to work. Those with emotional burdens found their way to a lightness of being. "For the first time in fifty-eight years, I AM FREE," exclaimed one intern. Another said that with Jack's guidance, she found "the courage to stop doubting." Still another commented, "Instead of making me reliant on him, Jack gave me the tools with which it became possible for me to heal myself."

The Discovery of Life's Purpose

One of my greatest achievements was the discovery of my life's purpose to be a master map maker. I realized I was to set down for others the map I was following to achieve meaning and abundance for myself.

Writing this book, then, is a major part of my life's purpose. It is the beginning of a series of maps that I'm planning to create to help people find their way to enrichment, enlightenment and self-empowerment.

I don't imagine I have to tell you what a magnificent feeling it is to know we are on earth for a reason and that we have the ability to achieve our purpose. Knowing our life's purpose is the starting point of all achievement. Once I understood this, I could get to know myself. Sound like a simple task? Self-knowledge can be the most elusive goal of all.

Each self is a distinct and unique entity, precious to the universal intelligence. Most of us, however, have developed a strong ego, which bears the responsibility for separating us from each other and the rest of the world. The ego tends to identify our self with our physical body. And the ego blocks out the underlying, unchanging personal essence that defines each of us. Actually experiencing and getting to know our essence is one of the highs of this life.

You may very well be skeptical of what I'm saying here. I'm not asking you to take my claims on faith. You are going to be given a way to test everything. When you follow our tested programs, you'll find they lead you to the abundant life, the overflowing life, the life we all desire and were put on this earth to experience. Such a life can be yours—not for the taking, but for the *doing*.

All of the material in this book is experiential. That means you actually put it into practice and see for yourself what you can achieve. You put it to work as you go through the interactive chapters. When you use the meditations of Chapters Four through Eight in your life, and they bring what you wish, then you don't guess or hope. You *know* they work for you.

I increased my personal power by quantum amounts. Not only did I begin to achieve more and more of my life goals, but success became predictable, almost inevitable. And as I bubbled over with the joy of such success, I had an irresistible urge to share the way to achieve it. With this book as your guide, you can construct and scientifically prove your own program. Use it, live it and watch in wonder as it changes your life.

May your journey be as miraculous as mine!

Sanford "Buddy" Frumker

CONTENTS

Foreword ix

Preface: An Invitation to a Life of Abundance xiii
A synthesis of East and West ◆ The mind-body continuum ◆ A direct message ◆ An answer to a life-long riddle ◆ "Renounce and enjoy" ◆ Restoration of physical health ◆ Boost to financial health ◆ Framework for everyone ◆ The discovery of life's purpose

1. *An Introduction to Applied Active Meditation* 1
A scientific method ◆ The test of increased abundance ◆ Abundance through the universal mind ◆ Sea of electromagnetic radiation ◆ Creative energy ◆ Regulating energy ◆ An alternative model ◆ The comprehensible universe ◆ The laws of thermodynamics ◆ Newton's laws of motion ◆ Movement toward evolution and harmony ◆ Why meditate? ◆ The power of the total mind ◆ Conscious mind ◆ Subconscious mind ◆ Paraconscious mind ◆ Measuring the mind's functions ◆ Two paraconscious functions ◆ Action: an essential connection ◆ Excitement: energy in motion ◆ The circuit of self-empowerment ◆ Learning total mind power ◆ How to use this program

2. *Living Your Journal* 22
Some suggestions about form ◆ Log Sheet: applied active meditation ◆ Scoring your attainment ◆ Appropriate and inappropriate forces ◆ Transcendence ◆ Discovering the direction of your life

3. *Breathing to Alter States of Consciousness* 31
The six levels of breathing ◆ Breathing rhythms and states
of consciousness ◆ Breathing exercises ◆ Breathing and
repression of feelings ◆ The right breathing pattern for
you ◆ The excitement factor

4. *The Cosmic Review* 44
The law of equivalent returns ◆ What the cosmic review can
do ◆ You are the expert ◆ Creating your horizon ◆ Letting
the day's events roll ◆ Examples of real life cosmic reviews
◆ Devaluing inappropriate actions ◆ Your journal ◆ A
summary of the steps in the cosmic review

5. *Psycho-physical Rehearsal* 57
From the universal to the personal ◆ Psycho-physical rehearsal, an experience of the mind ◆ Access to a great source
of information ◆ Psycho-physical rehearsal, part one—more
power now ◆ Psycho-physical rehearsal, part two—more
power for the future ◆ Steps in psycho-physical rehearsal,
part two ◆ Review and summary of the psycho-physical
rehearsal of future events ◆ More power and radiance ◆ The
fallacy of aging ◆ Thought patterns and psycho-physical
rehearsal ◆ Process: the most important part ◆ The experience of spontaneity ◆ The experience of non-attachment ◆
Reaction versus response ◆ Repetition, repetition, repetition ◆ Facing a hostile environment ◆ The importance of
intent ◆ Competence and spontaneity ◆ The mind's habitat
◆ Summaries ◆ A reminder

6. *Autogenic Psycho-physical Rehearsal* 80
Moving beyond the conscious mind ◆ Expanding the use of
your mind ◆ Exercises in using the autogenic psycho-
physical rehearsal: walking, swimming, talk show ◆ Healing
with the autogenic psycho-physical rehearsal ◆ The sequence
of meditations

7. *Guided Meditation* 98
The cosmic review and psycho-physical rehearsals ◆ The
guided meditation ◆ Becoming whole ◆ You have all the
answers ◆ The guided meditation process ◆ The formal
steps ◆ Guided meditations: the clay statue, the mountain
exercise, river and cavern exercise, the cube and sphere, the

seven door exercise ◆ Suggestions for further meditations ◆ Living every day of your life as a guided meditation

8. *Creative Meditation* 121
The meaning of enlightenment ◆ The concept of service to others ◆ The permanent creative principle ◆ Blockages to enlightenment ◆ Creative meditation ◆ The formal steps ◆ Candle flame meditation ◆ A journey of becoming

9. *Steps Toward a Co-creative Life* 132
Understanding and growing toward illumination ◆ The act of co-creation ◆ How the pieces of applied active meditation work together ◆ Four basic techniques for meditation ◆ Key concept: Transcendence ◆ Transcending positive events ◆ Bringing "God" into view

10. *The Applied Active Meditation Paradigm* 141

Suggested Reading 147

Index 150

1

AN INTRODUCTION TO
APPLIED ACTIVE MEDITATION

> *I give you the end of a golden string;*
> *Only wind it into a ball,*
> *It will lead you in at heaven's gate,*
> *Built in Jerusalem's wall.*
> —William Blake, "The Everlasting Gospel"

You are about to embark on a sojourn that will change your life. This journey will lead you to fulfill your highest destiny, to live in health and abundance and to soar to heights you never imagined possible. The point of this journey is the bringing of the universal mind into your everyday life.

Applied active meditation is the most effective known method of interacting with the universal mind and bringing its powers into our mind and self. With daily applied active meditation, you can put the enormous wisdom, insight and power of the universal mind to use in your personal life.

The universal mind is the power that created the entire universe, including you. Soon you will be using this power routinely. It will impact everything you do, every action you take. You will grow in power and awareness, and you will come to know your life's purpose.

What can I tell you about the universal mind? I can explain that it is everywhere, surrounding you completely and moving within you. Up until now you have been severely limited in your ability to perceive the universal mind. With the exercises in this book, you will expand your perception. You will learn how to use every part of your mind and to express its power in your life. Through the use of

1

applied active meditation, you will come in contact with the universal mind, and incorporate its intelligence into your daily life. The Jack Schwarz method has been perfected over twenty-five years of practical application. It has brought health and abundance to thousands. Now you also can be among those who profit from its practice.

A Scientific Method

Applied active meditation has its basis in science. It builds on the laws of the universe that human science has discovered and teaches you to move in accordance with these universal laws.

Most of the great discoveries of science have come through the rigorous testing of models called hypotheses. A hypothesis is something not yet proved but assumed to be true for the purposes of further study or investigation. Scientists construct hypotheses in order to predict outcomes. When the predicted outcomes consistently occur, the hypothesis is said to be scientifically valid.

In this book, you will scientifically test each applied active meditation (AAM) you do. As you proceed through the interactive chapters, you will use meditations to devise plans of action for your daily life. The consistent, predictable success you achieve through your actions will scientifically validate the process. You can never know truth by reading about it. The only way to know truth is to experience it.

The Test of Increased Abundance

The predictable outcome of the use of AAM is increased abundance. You will actually begin to achieve abundance for yourself as you apply the first meditations to your life. When each meditation consistently brings you abundance, you will have proven its validity. Each meditation will help you to build within yourself that knowledge and those powers that will bring you more abundance.

When I talk about abundance, I mean an overflowing fullness, a richness in all areas of your life. We have been taught to think about abundance only in the material sense. Obviously, financial and physical health are important aspects of an abundant life. But the kind of abundance I'm offering you includes emotional, mental and spiritual riches, too. A life of abundance is a life with direction and purpose. Discovering your life's purpose and living it is what the late Joseph Campbell so beautifully called "living your bliss." Living your bliss is living abundantly.

Applied active meditation is not something you sit in a corner and do for an hour each day. It is a method of living your life so that each day adds to your wisdom, power and abundance. It is a daily program, all day long, for achieving happiness and health.

AAM leads to immediate action in your everyday life. Your life is the testing laboratory for the effectiveness of the meditation method. As you test each meditation and prove the process valid, your life will become continually more exciting, with each day offering new opportunities. Abundance will become a predictable part of your life.

Abundance Through the Universal Mind

An abundant life comes through contact and interaction with the universal mind. When you add the unlimited power of the universal mind to your personal self, you achieve the means to abundance.

What is the universal mind? How do we know it exists? According to what laws does it operate?

The universal mind is the intelligence that designed and created the universe and is now operating it. The universe functions in accordance with strict laws. Nothing occurs by chance. You yourself are the best proof of the existence of the universal mind. You are made-up of approximately 72 trillion cells that work together to keep you functioning. Each of these parts is a complete factory in itself, far more complex than any computer or instrument humans have managed to build. Each cell performs over one million chemical reactions every second. And each cell has to interact perfectly with the other 72 trillion cells during these millions of reactions per second. For your cells to operate as a unit requires incredible intelligence. Where does this intelligence come from, and how is it communicated and carried?

Sea of Electromagnetic Radiation

Science has demonstrated that we live in a universe we can barely comprehend through our five physical senses. The material universe, the part to which our physical senses have access, is a small portion of the total universe—between two and four percent. The other ninety-six to ninety-eight percent of the universe is energy in the form of electromagnetic radiation. Almost all of this energy is invisible to our physical senses. The great English physicist, James Clerk Maxwell, demonstrated the existence of this sea of electromagnetic radiation. In his electromagnetic theory, published in 1867, Maxwell presented four equations to explain the workings of electricity and magnetism and to prove they were two inseparable aspects of one phenomenon—electromagnetic radiation.

Our physical bodies mirror the universe. To our senses, they seem to be solid matter. But when we examine our "solid" matter, we discover the same proportion of matter to energy. Our bodies, like all other matter in the universe, are composed of atoms. Only two percent of the atom is matter—the center with positively charged protons and neutrons and the negatively charged electrons circling the center. Between the center or nucleus of the atom and its electrons is a great deal of space, the other ninety-eight percent. We used to call this empty. Today we know this space is electromagnetic energy. We have instruments with which we can detect, map and measure this energy.

Throughout the universe, then, is a uniform electromagnetic field, filling all space that is not matter. This universal electromagnetic field surrounds us and moves within our bodies. It is a measurable phenomenon and a creative principle. The work of two scientists, in particular, has shown just how this energy orders life.

Creative Energy

Dr. Harold Saxton Burr, who taught neuroanatomy at the Yale University School of Medicine for nearly fifty years, investigated what he called the electric patterns of life. In 1972, he published a breakthrough work called *Blueprint for Immortality*.

Burr discovered that all material forms, including human bodies, are ordered and controlled by "electro-dynamic fields which can be measured and mapped with precision." Inherent in these fields, he said, is the power to direct the growth and development of any living system.

Burr called the electro-dynamic fields that he measured "L Fields," meaning life fields. "Until modern instruments revealed the existence of the controlling L Fields," he wrote, "biologists were at a loss to explain how our bodies 'keep in shape' through ceaseless metabolism and changes of material."

From modern research with "tagged" elements, we know the material of our bodies is constantly in flux. For example, all the protein in your body is turned over every six months. If I do not see you for six months, when we meet again, I will not see one molecule that was there six months earlier. Yet the new molecules are put together in such a way that they form exactly you and you alone, and I easily recognize you.

You make a new skin once a month, a new skeleton every three months, a new stomach lining every five days. You have a functionally new liver every six weeks. The carbon, hydrogen, nitrogen and oxygen of your brain cells are replaced every year. The raw material of your DNA, which controls all the functions of your physical body, is replaced every six weeks. Ninety-eight percent of the atoms and molecules that make up your physical body are replaced every year.

Think of it—over the course of a year, your physical body dies away almost completely. Yet you live on. Look at photographs of yourself over the years. The differences in your looks as you grow older are obvious. No matter what your age, you are still obviously you. What is it that keeps you the same person in spite of such large changes?

There is some part of you that did not die when your physical body did. That something not only replaced your dead atoms and molecules, it put the new ones together into exactly you and you alone. That something is the creative energy field that forms you into a unique being. As Burr put it, "The electro-dynamic field of the body serves as a matrix or mold, which preserves the arrangement and activities and functions of the body."

Regulating Energy

After years of mapping and measuring L Fields, Burr declared that the essence of a human being is pure energy. His conclusions have been verified and amplified by the work of Dr. Fritz-Albert Popp, a German physicist who has, in Munich, the largest biophoton laboratory in the world. Using a photon multiplier as his chief measuring instrument, Popp has shown that every cell in the human body communicates with every other cell by means of electro-magnetic radiation. Popp's research provides further evidence that the physiological functions of living organisms are controlled and regulated by electromagnetic field patterns.

Photons are packages of energy. Biophotons are packages of energy transmitted by living organisms. Popp found that biophotons are electromagnetic waves with high frequencies. He also discovered that in the human body DNA has the role of absorbing and transmitting biophotons. Thus DNA controls the biochemical and physiological reactions of every cell.

DNA does this by sending out "written" instructions in the form of RNA. When the electromagnetic field is correct, DNA keeps the body functioning correctly through its RNA messages. When the electromagnetic field is interfered with, DNA sends out faulty messages, and the body functions incorrectly. Thus, at a basic level, the cause of any disease is incorrect information resulting from an interfered with electromagnetic field pattern. When cancer cells grow wild and destroy instead of cooperating, they have, as Popp puts it, "lost the possibility of taking up mutual photons from each other."

According to Dr. Popp, the universal electromagnetic field is the base for cell communication. "It is the most fundamental base of communication, because it works between all the cells, between all the single systems of cells. Between all molecules with the highest speed which is possible. The speed of light."

Scientific research has shown that pure energy creates and controls us. I call this energy the universal mind. Some call this universal electromagnetic field God. Some call it Buddha. Some call it the void or the unified field. You choose your own terminology.

What I am calling the universal mind has the power to put together atoms, then molecules and, finally, the unique living form that is you. Universal energy built the entire universe and is responsible for keeping it functioning. You are built by the universal mind, and you are kept alive and functioning by universal intelligence. With applied active meditation we convert the power of the universal mind into our own personal power. It is the greatest source of power available to us on earth, and you will learn to use it in your life, beginning with Chapter Four of this book.

An Alternative Model

Despite all that modern physics has demonstrated about the creative energy that operates in the world, Western society persists in emphasizing the material at the expense of the non-material. We have been taught to rely on our physical senses as our only source of information. We have been taught that unless we can weigh or measure something, it doesn't exist. We have been taught we are nothing more than our physical body and that, as an individual material being, we are separate from all other people, animals and objects in the universe.

As a result of this view of the universe, the world is becoming a soulless place. Life has lost much of its meaning. People are suffering from the effects of living lives based on alienation, loneliness, stress, disease, anxiety and fear. The ills of society are so deeply rooted they seem impossible to cure. But to accept these ills in order to live a life of convenience is to surrender any possibility of meaning, and to rule out the achievement of total abundance.

I believe there is a more rewarding model, one that can lead to unity and wholeness, one that will bring meaning to our lives. Obviously, we are more than our physical body. The material parts of our body are constantly changing. Yet we remain the same person. The creative energy field that holds you together in a recognizable form is your essence. Your essence is unchanging. It is the same energy that fills the universe, but it has individualized to form you.

The Comprehensible Universe

The universal mind operates according to certain laws. As Albert Einstein said, "The most incomprehensible thing about the universe is its comprehensibility." We can indeed understand how our universe works. Our science has discovered certain laws that predict the way matter is created and the way energy interacts with matter. These laws also apply to the interactions between the universal mind and our physical selves. It is by understanding and obeying these laws that we become complete and discover our purpose in life.

The Laws of Thermodynamics

The first laws that we need to understand are the laws of thermodynamics. These two laws give us incredible insight into what life *is*. They contain the overall picture of the meaning of our temporal life on earth and our eternal life in the universe.

The first law of thermodynamics states that energy can never be created or destroyed. Energy is conserved. The total amount of energy remains constant.

Since each of us is a unique individual physical body, each of us had to have been created by a unique energy field. The unique energy field that created, and *is* us, could not have been made since energy cannot be created. The only way our unique creative energy field could have come into existence was by separating from the universal creative energy that fills the universe and our self. A very tiny portion of universal creative energy was transformed into the unique energy field that produced your physical body. That unique energy field is you and you alone. It is your essence.

As research like Dr. Burr's has shown, your essence is pure energy. Therefore it does not age, and cannot be destroyed. It remains a permanent part of the universe. Once Dr. Burr confirmed the existence of our individualized creative electromagnetic fields, he told us we are immortal. You have a unique energy field that is eternal. You are an eternal self.

The second law of thermodynamics states that any closed system that uses energy always goes from a more organized to a less organized form. Whenever energy is used to perform any work, most of it is used in performing the work, but some of it is always lost into the atmosphere and cannot be recovered. Thus whenever we do any work, or take any action, some energy is irretrievably lost. There is less energy available after the work is completed than there was at the beginning.

A common example is the light bulb. Electrical energy is used to heat the filament until it glows and radiates light. However, some of the energy turns into heat and is lost into the environment. We can know this is true by touching a light bulb that has been burning for any length of time. Eventually, due to the loss of energy, the bulb burns out.

According to the second law, closed systems that do work—and we all are closed systems that do work—move from order to disorder. In time any closed system will become a disordered system. The word the scientists use to describe this increase of disorder is "entropy." In all closed systems over a period of time entropy increases. Disorder always increases; it never decreases. Every appliance or automobile reaches such a state of disorder that it ceases to function.

Your physical body is a closed system; therefore every day it becomes more of a disordered system. When disorder reaches the level at which your physical body ceases to function, we call it death and imply an ending; but, in fact, the physical body is doing nothing more than following the second law of thermodynamics.

The first law states that energy cannot be created or destroyed and is eternal. However, all the matter in the universe, including our physical selves, experiences entropy and is, consequently, temporary. Thus our temporal body must stop functioning. But our eternal self, since it is energy, continues on. Our eternal self cannot be destroyed because it is pure energy.

Why does the universal mind separate unique energy fields from itself and create temporal beings?

Universal creative energy is totally impersonal. It fills the universe and is the same everywhere. However, change and evolution are constant activities of energy. Universal energy evolves by separating from itself packages of individualized creative energy. It creates components that have the capacity to evolve to higher levels. The universal mind creates us in order to evolve itself to higher levels.

Newton's Laws of Motion

Energy is always in motion. The laws governing this motion were first described by Sir Isaac Newton. Newton's first law of motion says, "Every body continues in its state of rest, or of uniform motion in a straight line, unless it is compelled to change that state by forces impressed on it."

Applying this law of motion to our lives on this earth, we can know that everything that happens to us is the result of the specific actions we take. Our actions are the equivalent of Newton's forces. Far more effective than trying to correct a specific problem we're having, is to change our actions that are *causing* the problem. Through this book, we will learn which of our actions are appropriate for us and conducive to abundance, and which are inappropriate and getting in the way of abundance.

Newton's second law states, "Force equals mass times acceleration." This is the law that lets us know of our capacity for controlling the quality of the forces being applied to our lives. Since mass and acceleration are easily changed, then the force that is their result is mutable as well. This means that once you understand the forces affecting your life, you have the power to change them. The process of applied active meditation you are about to learn will enable you to take control of the forces influencing all areas of your life.

Newton's third law states, "For every action, there is an equal and opposite reaction." This tells us we live in a bipolar universe, that the forces affecting us come in opposite pairs. That is to say, every force in our life immediately produces another force that is opposite to it. This is one of the most important laws for you to apply to your daily life. Because of it, you can be sure whenever you experience something that produces negative or harmful effects in your life, there is available an opposing something that will produce positive and healthy effects.

The universe is neither good nor bad. It is both good *and* bad simultaneously. A major aim of the program of applied active meditation is the development of your ability to tune into the positive force that goes along with any negative one you may be experiencing. When you use AAM you deactivate the negative force and bring its positive opposite into play.

Movement Toward Evolution and Harmony

By putting the laws of thermodynamics and those of motion together, we know the universe is in a constant state of motion and change. This change wants to be in the direction of evolution, of becoming more. You cannot stop this constant change, but you can influence it. You are in charge of the amount and direction of the change that takes place through you. If you direct your changes toward growth and evolution, you will be moving in accord with the universe. If you resist evolution, you will be at odds with the universe.

Every change in the universe also aims at achieving harmony. When your actions increase harmony in the universe, you are contributing toward universal harmony. When your actions disrupt harmony, you are disrupting universal harmony.

Your job in this life is to obey the universal laws and move your life in the direction of evolution and harmony. Your eternal self is a package of individualized creative energy that has the potential for growth. Because through you it has taken on physical form, your eternal self now can communicate with both the material world and the universal mind. By combining your daily material experiences with the universal mind, you can accomplish the job for which you were created. In the process, you will achieve the highest abundance possible on earth! When the time comes for your body to cease functioning, you take nothing material with you. You will, however, take all the universal mind you have accumulated.

Who, What and Why Are We?

Who are we? Where did we come from? Why are we here? There is nothing *more important* in your life than your answers to these questions. Your answers will flow through every meditation in this book, and most important, through every part of your life.

The research of physics and the two laws of thermodynamics have shown us that the material world is created by energy. Einstein's famous formula E=MC squared expresses this fact.

Therefore, since each of our human bodies is material, each of us is created by an energy source. Since every human being is different from every other human being, every one of us has been created by an energy source that is unique to each of us.

Most of us have been taught to believe we are our physical body. But our physical body is always changing. All the protein in your body is replaced every six months. You make a new skin once a month, a new skeleton every three months and a new stomach lining every five days. The carbon, hydrogen and oxygen of your brain are replaced every year.

Every seven years every single atom in your body and every single part of you dies and is replaced. But you are still you. Look at photographs of yourself at ages 10, 20, 30, etc. Each photograph is very different from the preceding one, but they are all you. If you are your body, which picture is you, because they are all very different? *Think of it—over the course of seven years your body completely dies, yet you live on!* Obviously you are more than just your body.

You were not created only at conception, you are continually being created every second. If you were only your physical body, your life would be extremely short. You are both your physical body and the energy source that created it. As explained by the two laws of thermodynamics, your body—which is material—is temporary and is always physically deteriorating. However, your energy source is permanent. It can never be destroyed, it can only be transformed.

How then did the energy source that is you come into existence? Energy cannot be created. Energy creates matter, not more energy. Therefore, where did your energy source come from?

The only way it could have come into existence was to have separated from the universal creative energy, the universal energy that is our creator. Our western world calls it God; it has thousands of other names. In order for each of us to be, our creator separated from itself tiny energy sources designed for the creation of each of us. Each of us is a separation from our creator, yet each of us is a little bit of our creator!

Why then was our physical body created? Why are we here?

Our creator already is and has everything. Our creator cannot evolve to anything more. However, the universal law of evolution tells us that the universe "He" created is always changing and evolving into more, into higher levels of being. The only way our universe and its creator can become more is by having parts of it become more. We are each a part of the universe. Therefore, whenever we become more, whenever we evolve into more, the entire universe evolves into more. The mission of each of us on earth is to use our temporary human life to evolve to our highest possible level, and by so doing evolve the entire universe to a higher level.

We can do this because our life on earth is a co-creational experience. Our energy source originally created us. Since our energy source is energy and therefore eternal, we call it our eternal self, or our essence. Now, during our life on earth, our mission is to evolve our eternal self to the highest level possible. How do we do that? Each time we evolve our human self to a higher level, we also evolve our eternal self to a higher level. This will be discussed more in Chapter 8.

Our earth life is our means for achieving a richer existence for our eternal self and our eternal life. However, you will find that in so doing you will also achieve the richest possible life for yourself on earth. A life of evolution for our eternal self is a life of bliss for our trip on earth.

The meditations you are about to learn will be your step-by-step guide to wealth and joy on earth. But they are not our end goal. They are the means to achieving the highest possible evolution of our eternal self to greater and greater levels of being. When our "life" on earth ceases, our eternal self will be far more evolved than when it began. That is the purpose and mission of our life on earth. When our life on earth ends, our eternal self is ready to move ahead full speed into a much more exciting next step in our eternal journey. When you get to Chapter 4, you will take your first big step in this journey. You are now on your way.

Why Meditate?

Meditation, as used in this book, is a practical guide to utilizing the total mind to achieve total abundance. Aryeh Kaplan, in his magnificent book, *Jewish Meditation: A Practical Guide,* poignantly sums up why we should meditate and what we can achieve by applied active meditation.

He first states that you might find yourself thinking about such fundamental questions as:

What do I ultimately want out of life?
What gives life meaning?
What is the meaning of life in general?
If I had my life to live over, what would I do with it?
What ideals, if any, would I be willing to die for?
What would bring me more happiness than anything else in the
    world?

To these questions, Rabbi Kaplan answers, "As you explore what is most meaningful to you, you may come to a point where you feel that you are reaching a new threshold. You may find yourself pondering not only the meaning of your own life, but the very meaning of existence in general. At this point, you will have discovered God."

Rabbi Kaplan concludes, "Once a person discovers God in this manner, he might want to transform his meditation into a conversation with God. If one discovers God as the ultimate depth of one's being, then the way to relate to this depth would be to relate to God. At this point one's meditation into the meaning of existence might become a silent conversation with God."

In these two paragraphs Rabbi Kaplan has described the essence of what you will discover in Chapters Four through Eight. I also recommend reading all of his wonderful book.

The Power of the Total Mind

Your mind is the conduit between yourself and the universal mind. It is also the connection between your eternal self and your physical body. Your mind fills and surrounds your body and extends well beyond it. Through the use of your total mind, you can achieve your life's purpose, which is bringing the power of the universal mind to your eternal self.

When I talk about your total mind, I am referring to a tripartite entity. You may not be fully aware of these three distinctly different functions: the conscious, the paraconscious and the subconscious. Your conscious mind communicates with the material world. Your paraconscious mind communicates with the universal mind. And your subconscious mind stores all the information from both the material world and the universal mind—then combines this information into your plans, dreams, desires, awareness and the eventual actions you take.

The point of the exercises in this book is to develop the use of your paraconscious mind so you can incorporate its input into the actions you take in your life.

Conscious Mind

Your *conscious* mind depends on the five physical senses for its basic information. It is the part that is in contact with the material world. With its thinking and reasoning powers, your conscious mind produces words to describe what your five physical senses are telling it. The reasoning power of your conscious mind is what makes you human. This power is both your greatest distinction and the worst obstacle to the fulfillment of your life's purpose. Depending on the rational mind alone leads to a perception of separateness and isolation. Ego is a product of your conscious mind, and it creates the perception that you are an individual entity, separate from all else in the universe.

Each day your conscious mind is bombarded with millions of stimuli. If your conscious mind tried to respond to, or even be aware of most of these stimuli, you would not survive. The onslaught would be too great. When this torrent of sensations hits, the conscious mind has to decide which to allow in and which to block out.

Your conscious mind acts according to belief systems you have formulated. The subconscious stores all the information brought to it and fits that information into patterns that define your way of looking at the world. Once these patterns are in place, your conscious mind chooses to see and experience only those stimuli and ideas that correspond to and reinforce your belief systems. Your conscious mind reflects what you believe is the reality and truth of the world you live in. It guides your actions according to the belief systems that control it.

Subconscious Mind

The *subconscious* mind functions as the archives or library of your total self. All the input from the conscious mind is permanently registered here. The subconscious mind then forms relationships between the contents of these archives and develops plans of action and reaction. This means whenever you want to do anything, your subconscious mind takes information from its archives and sends instructions to the conscious mind on what to do, how to do it and how to feel about it.

Your conscious and subconscious minds work as a team. Stimulus A enters your conscious mind. You respond with B. Therefore Stimulus A is paired with Response B in your subconscious archives. When your conscious mind next encounters Stimulus A, your subconscious mind will prompt you to respond with B.

From your subconscious archives comes your instruction book on life. The *cards* you have in this file determine the wideness or narrowness of the life you live, its success or failure, its health or disease, its misery or bliss.

For most people, the belief systems put together in the subconscious mind build a prison, limiting awareness and shutting out possibilities. Their experience is similar to the voluntary confinement of flies that have been in a jar with a lid on it. Once these flies have tried to get out of the jar and encountered the lid enough times, they give up. Even when the lid is removed, most of the flies will remain in the jar. Based on their experience of hitting the lid, the flies reduce the size of their reality to the confines of the jar. Most people have constructed lids over their lives.

The same phenomenon has been demonstrated with fish. Put fish in a large tank and in the middle of the tank place a piece of glass separating the two halves. After a number of days, remove the glass. Most of the fish will continue to live in only their half of the tanks.

There have been more sophisticated studies done about the limitations that the teaming of the conscious and subconscious minds can impose. At Harvard, an experiment was done with cats and different kinds of stimuli. One group of kittens was raised in a room that had only horizontal stripes. Another group was raised in a room with only vertical stripes. When the kittens grew up, the horizontal stripe group could not see the vertical legs of a chair that was placed in the room. Examination of these cats' brains showed they did not have the connections between neurons to see vertical stimuli. Likewise, the vertical stripe group could not see horizontal lines; their brains never developed the connections that would have allowed them to detect horizontals.

Studies like the one done at Harvard prove that the mechanics of perception are such that your initial sensory exposures and how you interpret them actually develop a nervous system designed to see only that to which it was exposed in the first place. Research by Candace Pert has shown that each thought creates a specific neurotransmitter which helps to determine *how* a nervous system will respond and *what* it will respond to.

Therefore, if you have not been exposed to a specific stimulus, or if it has not been interpreted for you in a certain way, it does *not exist* for you. The Buddhist law of Maya, which is the law of illusion, speaks of the limitations of perception. Maya does not say that the material world is an illusion. Rather, the illusion is our belief that the small part of universal reality of which we are aware is the whole picture. What we perceive is indeed real, but it is only a *small part* of reality. And it is not the essential reality. Our personal reality is the lid on top of our jar.

Today we have built a model of so-called scientific biology based on the illusion that the world is only made-up of material objects, each one individual and separated from each other in time and space. We are like the Harvard cats, except instead of vertical or horizontal stripes, we use data, measurements and things we call facts to define our reality. We are not wrong. But we aren't right either. We do not see the whole picture. So much more is available to us when we learn how to expand our awareness and use our total mind.

Paraconscious Mind

This brings us to the third function of the mind: the *paraconscious mind*, the function that is in contact with the universal mind. Paraconscious means beyond the conscious. Society does little to encourage recognition of the paraconscious function. In fact, most of the experts will tell you the paraconscious mind is a delusion. Once you personally experience the paraconscious mind, however, you will know that your mind has three functions. And you will know how to use all three of them.

With your paraconscious mind, you can directly experience and communicate with the universal mind! This means you can also add universal intelligence to your subconscious archives. The insight and power in the universal mind is far, far greater than anything your consciously-processed data could add.

When you learn to recognize your paraconscious mind and to acknowledge that through it you are in touch with the universal mind, you will experience a quantum increase in power and effectiveness. By adding the input of your paraconscious mind to that of your conscious mind, your life will attain new dimensions. Your possibilities will become virtually unlimited!

Measuring the Mind's Functions

Scientific evidence for the three functions of the mind comes from the measurement of the electrical impulses produced by the brain. As the live brain functions, its nerve cells generate electrical impulses. These impulses are emitted as waves, and this electrical activity can be measured.

Two measurements can be made of each brain wave. First is frequency, which determines the length of brain waves and is measured in cycles per second (cps). The lower the frequency—the fewer the cps—the longer the brain wave.

Secondly, we can measure the strength or power of each wave. We do this in terms of amplitude or the height of each wave. The more powerful a wave, the greater its amplitude or height. The amplitude of brain waves is measured in micro volts.

Brain waves are grouped into four main types according to their frequencies. From the highest to the lowest, these frequencies are known as beta, alpha, theta and delta brain waves. Beta is 13 to approximately 40 cps. Alpha is 8 to 13 cps. Theta is 4 to 8 cps. And delta is 0 to 4 cps.

The different types of brain waves correspond to different functions of the mind. The conscious mind expresses itself through beta waves. The subconscious mind expresses itself through alpha waves. The paraconscious mind produces both theta and delta waves.

Two Paraconscious Functions

When the paraconscious mind is producing delta waves, it is deeply tuned in to the universal mind. The lower the frequency, the deeper the wave goes into the universal mind. At 1 cps, each brain wave is 186,282 miles long. This means that each brain wave is in contact with the universal mind within 186,282 miles of the person radiating that brain wave. Obviously, at 1 cps, the paraconscious will communicate with far more of the universal mind than at 8 cps.

However, when functioning in delta, our paraconscious mind cannot communicate with our subconscious mind. In delta, our paraconscious mind is non-verbal. Our subconscious mind needs words and images. This is where the theta function of the paraconscious mind kicks in. Operating at theta, our paraconscious mind transforms the universal mind of the delta level into a form that can enter the subconscious archives.

The universal mind is a much greater intelligence than your conscious mind. The universal mind brings information and insights that are not available to the conscious mind. Almost every one of you has experienced this. In today's psychology, delta is called deep sleep, and theta is called pre-sleep.

How many times have you consciously tried to solve a problem for hours with no results? You go to sleep. Your conscious mind is no longer at work, but your paraconscious mind is. You wake up suddenly at 5 A.M. with the answer.

One of the most famous examples of this is how Thomas Edison invented the electric light bulb. He tried repeatedly to find a filament that would not burn up when he heated it enough to produce light. Then one night in his sleep, with his conscious mind turned off, his paraconscious mind was able to show him charcoal being made. Reportedly, he immediately saw the answer to his problem. The process that makes charcoal from coal keeps the available oxygen low so that the coal doesn't burn up. Edison removed the oxygen from the light bulb, and the heated filament glowed and gave light for eight hours before burning up.

The light bulb was invented by the paraconscious input of Thomas Edison.

Your conscious mind, which is strongly verbal in all its images and experiences, has a direct line to your subconscious archives. That line is far stronger than the line from your paraconscious mind. Therefore, as long as you are using the input of your conscious mind, you cannot receive paraconscious information. Thus to add the intelligence of the universal mind to your archives, you must shut down your conscious input and tune in to your paraconscious mind. You will learn to do this as you proceed through this book.

Action: an Essential Connection

Adding the intelligence of the universal mind to the archives of our subconscious is only the first connection on what I call the *circuit of self-empowerment*. The essential second connection is spontaneous action in accordance with this new input. Unless we act on the new input from the universal mind, it will pass through and be gone. We must act rapidly on the paraconscious input without letting in the questions and doubts of the conscious mind.

As pointed out above, your actions are controlled by your conscious mind. So when the intelligence of the universal mind comes to the subconscious mind, the subconscious mind prompts the conscious mind to act. Doubts or fears in the conscious mind will immediately stop all paraconscious input.

Excitement: Energy in Motion

In order to act immediately and spontaneously, you have to have power, which is another quantifiable aspect of your mind. Power is the micro voltage your brain produces.

The average person walking around in beta is operating with a micro voltage of 5 to 15. In alpha, theta or delta, the micro voltage is up between 45 and 55. However, for the paraconscious input to overcome the doubts and fears of the conscious mind and to spur it into creative action, the micro voltage has to be between 85 and 95.

So how *do* you get your micro voltage up? It flies when you totally desire something, when you become consumed with excitement. To transform universal power into personal power, you need excitement. Excitement is energy in motion. It is E Motion. Excitement is the greatest wealth you can have on this earth. Through sustained excitement, you have the power to add the intelligence of the universal mind to your subconscious archives.

As you go through this program and learn to use your total mind power, you will gain a sense of excitement that will give you the push needed to keep moving, changing, evolving. You will feel more alive and more aware than you have ever felt before.

The Circuit of Self-empowerment

The increase in power that you will experience is cumulative; it flows along a circuit that spirals ever upwards. First, your conscious mind is continually sending input from your daily life into your subconscious. Your paraconscious mind tunes into the universal mind and deposits information from the universal mind into your subconscious mind. Your subconscious mind then integrates the intelligence from the universal mind with the input of daily events and undergoes an immense increase in power. The subconscious mind uses its new strength and awareness to draw up plans for action in your daily life. The conscious mind now must put those plans into action without doubts, fears or changes in any way. Then the actions you take are much wiser and more powerful because of the integration that has occurred. And when you take action, the power of the universal mind becomes your own personal power. And so the upward spiral goes.

I call this continuous movement to higher levels the *circuit of self-empowerment*. Its four basic connections are:

1. Conscious mind input from your daily life

2. Paraconscious mind input from the universal mind

3. Formulation of plans in the subconscious mind

4. Action taken on those plans. (The action must be that devised by the paraconscious-subconscious mind interaction—without any changes by the doubts, fears, and belief systems of the conscious mind.)

At the end of each circuit, two things occur. First, the new power brought to you from the universal mind becomes a permanent part of you and is yours to use, whenever needed, for the rest of your life. This increased personal power is at your disposal each time you face new problems or have new desires you wish to achieve. *There is no known limit to the personal power that you can accumulate. Every time you use your total mind, you increase your personal power.* Whatever you add to your subconscious archives is there permanently. You never lose what you add because evolution is a one-way street. You can fail to use what is available to you, but you can never lose it.

The second thing that occurs is that once the circuit of self-empowerment is completed a new bit of the universal mind is added to your eternal self. Completing a circuit elevates your eternal self to a higher level. Whatever you gain from the universal mind is yours forever. When the time comes for your body to cease functioning, you will take nothing material with you. But you will take all the intelligence from the universal mind that you have accumulated. The question for your trip on earth is: *How much of the universal mind are you going to add to your eternal self?*

Learning Total Mind Power

You have the power to ensure that your eternal self—that individualized creative energy package which has separated from the universal mind to become you—will leave your material body at a much more evolved level than when your body was born.

As a human being, you have been given the ability to tune into the intelligence and power of the universe, to live side by side with your creator. To refuse to use this gift is to turn your back on your creator. To ignore this remarkable ability is to miss the purpose of life. You have been put on this earth to evolve, to move with the universal mind in its quest for growth and change. You can fulfill your earthly task only by learning to use your total mind. Only through the use of your total mind can you achieve the evolution that your eternal self and the universe require. Your practice of applied active meditation is not meant to be a limited, isolated segment of your daily life. It is a complete meditation that becomes a constant part of your everyday activities.

AAM takes practice and discipline. This book is arranged to encourage you to continue on the path of applied active meditation by letting you see the rewards right away. Remember, the first rewards are mere glimpses of the vast power you are beginning to tap into. The best is always yet to come.

Through the exercises here, you will learn:

1. How to use all the functions of your mind

2. How to greatly increase the power of your mind

3. And finally, how to use your total mind power in daily life to achieve abundance

How to Use This Program

I recommend you follow the exercises in the order they are presented. Please remember that knowledge for its own sake is of little value. Knowledge becomes valuable only when you build a model with it, and use that model to take action. Your model becomes valid only with successful use. Having a map is no substitute for actually walking the territory.

In the next chapter I talk about the advantages of keeping a journal during this experience. Consider this suggestion very carefully. We have found those students who keep a journal make much more progress toward abundant lives than those who don't.

The chapter on journal keeping is followed by one on breathing. Correct breathing will enhance your powers. For maximum results, this program requires that you learn how to breathe. Please pay close attention to the chapter on breathing and do all the exercises.

As you are learning to breathe, you can begin the exercises described in Chapter 4. Here is where you will learn to do the cosmic review, a process designed to show you the contents of your subconscious mind. If you find fears, doubts and questions in your mind, you will learn to replace them with courage, optimism and confidence. Cosmic review is a process of transformation by examination of past actions.

In Chapter 5, you'll discover the first two parts of the psycho-physical rehearsal, a program for filling your mind with images of success and then applying those expectations to your daily life. You will notice a great expansion in your personal powers and an increase in successful experiences.

In Chapter 6, you will learn to devise your own psycho-physical rehearsals, and by doing so, to use them for anything you wish—from routine activities and commonplace objects to all areas of your life.

Chapter 7 introduces the concept of guided meditation, in which you discover the themes or ideas that are important for you to work on.

And in Chapter 8, you practice creative meditation. Here you bring all the elements of total mind power together to reach the deepest levels of the universal mind.

With every step you will be gaining universal power and intelligence. As you assume these empowering attributes, you will change from a limited, fearful being to an expansive, excited, radiant self. You will know your place in the universe and be capable of amazing feats. Anything humanly possible will be possible for you.

I know this program works. You will soon know the same thing because you will prove the validity of the circuit of self-empowerment with every successful connection that you make. Access to the universal mind through your paraconscious mind will become normal. You will begin living abundantly, gaining significant new powers and using them to enrich your daily life.

Now you are ready to take your first steps on your path of action, your journey to your life's purpose and the source of all being.

2
LIVING YOUR JOURNAL

> *I was angry with my friend*
> *I told him my wrath, my wrath did end.*
> *I was angry with my foe:*
> *I told it not, my wrath did grow.*
> —William Blake, "A Poison Tree"

As you use this book to learn the process of applied active meditation, keeping a journal will greatly contribute toward your success. In fact, keeping a journal may be the only way you can succeed. It can be a written journal, a tape-recorded journal, or a combination of both. My experience with the Jack Schwarz program has shown those who fail to keep journals achieve very little, even though they attend workshops, read books, have peak experiences, and talk and talk and talk.

Applied active meditation is a process by which you use day-to-day happenings as stepping stones to increased personal power. In your subconscious, you integrate an event from your daily life with input from the universal mind. Then you put your new awareness to work by acting on it. Every time you complete a unit of this process, you have new powers. Thus the growth of your life and powers is a continuous process. But you do not increase these powers by reading books or taking workshops. You increase these powers only when you *live* them, only when you *act*.

Living your journal is one of the most powerful steps of self-development you will ever take. Just what do I mean by "living your journal?" Do you remember Newton's first law of motion, the law of inertia, which says we will all remain precisely where we are and go nowhere unless a force is applied? Keeping a journal is the force you need to overcome resistance to change. The act of writing in a journal puts you in the flow of your life and sets up a momentum that is virtually unstoppable.

A journal gives form to the experiences you have and lets you draw on them repeatedly for insight and greater depth. The events of your life, the meditations you do, the inner experiences you become aware of and the actions you take are all there in black and white, recorded with care and attention. Your journal reflects the motion of your experiences. Through the descriptive language in your journal, not only can you re-experience an event—you can also know the flow of thoughts, feelings, ecstasies, depressions, energy patterns, etc., that accompanied it. Your journal entries record the totality of any experience.

Reading your journal, you will begin to find a continuity through all your experiences. By making a note of that continuity each time you see it, your journal will keep you in touch with the thread that is running all through your life process. It will depict the direction and level of your self-evolution. By reading your entries, you can re-enter the flow of that process if you are feeling lost or stuck. The notes on continuity will encourage further movement of that process.

As you create your journal, your journal creates you! As your awareness and consciousness expand, you will expand your journal. And then your journal will further expand you.

Through AAM, you develop an inner momentum. Your journal entries make that process visible so you can feed on it. With each set of entries, you increase the motion of your life toward whatever direction you desire.

Some Suggestions about Form

I'm going to suggest the kinds of information you might want to record. Please understand, however, that I do not expect you to follow a rigid form. Each person is unique; your journal will reflect your individuality. Applied active meditation is a process through which all kinds of people—regardless of age, gender, culture, religion and education—can clarify their lives and develop their inner resources. It does not depend on any one belief system or doctrine. It's a process whereby you become even more your own person. Through AAM, you will discover your inner sense of truth and validate the realities of your own life. And you'll unleash within yourself resources you did not know you possessed. You'll draw universal power out of the distinct experiences of your life. You will recognize your own identity and self, and harmonize with the larger identity of the universe.

Your journal entries may change with the nature of the events you are recording, with the emotional or physical state your are in and with what you desire to achieve. The form that follows is merely a guide. Alter it to suit yourself. Ignore it if it isn't helpful to you. The form is meant to serve all phases of the applied active meditation process, beginning with the cosmic review.

Log Sheet: Applied Active Meditation

Event:
Date:
My target:
Attainment/score:
General feelings, achievements, doubts:
Appropriate perceptions and feelings and how they affected me and the process:

1. What do I think?
2. What do I feel?
3. What do I know?

Inappropriate perceptions and feelings and how they affected me and the process:

1. What do I think?
2. What do I feel?
3. What do I know?

How I transcended these inappropriate perceptions:

1. What do I think?
2. What do I feel?
3. What do I know?

On the first line of the form, briefly describe the event upon which you meditated. It may be a past, present or future activity from your daily life. Or, as you grow more proficient in the method, it may be a symbolic meditation.

After listing the event and the date on which the meditation occurred, write down your target, which is what you hoped to achieve from the meditation. Your target can be to solve a specific problem, to increase your income, to strengthen a relationship, etc.

Scoring Your Attainment

At the completion of the meditation, write what you attained by it on the line under the target line. Describe your attainment in words and give it a score; ten means complete achievement and zero means no movement at all. Your actual attainment may be different from your original target. If that is the case, write what you did attain and whether it was more desirable than your original goal. Record this in your score.

Remember that the emphasis in applied active meditation is on the *process* rather than on the specific goal. When you set a specific goal and focus on that goal alone, you limit what you can achieve. When you focus on the process, instead, your possible achievements are virtually unlimited. Focus on the process. You will almost invariably achieve your goal; and you will go beyond that goal to achieve successes that you have not yet dreamed of. Goals are limited to your past experiences. The process can take you to the new, the unexpected, the extraordinary.

Appropriate and Inappropriate Forces

After you have described the result of each meditation, use your journal to become aware of the forces that are pushing you toward positive action. Also be aware of their opposite—those forces of inertia that push back, saying, "Stay where you are and do nothing. Do not change. Change is risky and you are incompetent."

I give the label *appropriate* to those forces pushing toward success and growth. The forces keeping you back are *inappropriate*. Appropriate forces are excitement, zest, desire, faith, confidence, high self-esteem, etc. Inappropriate forces are fear, hate, bitterness, anger, low self-esteem, self-righteousness, etc. When you actually record the forces operating in your life, you immediately increase greatly the power of the appropriate ones and, at the same time, dramatically decrease the power of those that are inappropriate.

In listing appropriate and inappropriate forces, you need to take the three parts of your mind into account: 1. the conscious: what you think, 2. the subconscious: what you feel, and 3. the paraconscious: what you know. I also prefer to list all the appropriate forces in each category before going back and listing the inappropriate forces at work. It never hurts to accentuate the positive.

Category 1—The Conscious Mind: What do you think?

This input from your conscious mind is built on the experiences of your daily life and based on logical verification. In your journal, describe your thoughts prior to and during the meditation. First write down the thoughts that helped the process proceed and flow. Examples of these would be images of the target you have set or the action you would like to take.

Category 2—The Subconscious Mind: What do you feel?

Write about what you feel emotionally and also what you feel inside your body. What areas feel strong? Where do you experience a powerful energy flow? What parts of you feel hot? Which parts of you feel vibrant and healthy? Describe as much as you can about your emotions and your feelings. The greater your awareness of these things, the greater your power to be in control of your life.

Category 3—The Paraconscious Mind: What do you know?

Knowing comes only from experience. Knowing occurs when your paraconscious mind brings intelligence from the universal mind into your subconscious mind—which, in turn, integrates this new information with all the input that has preceded it. The subconscious mind then presents new and more powerful plans of action to your conscious mind. And your conscious mind puts these plans to work in your daily life. The result is the circuit of self-empowerment, one of the most powerful processes available to any human being.

When you get to this category, you will see that writing in your journal is just the action you need to complete a circuit of self-empowerment. By the act of writing, you are putting intelligence from the universal mind to work in your daily life. Your perspective on the meditation you have just completed is dramatically new because of the knowledge your subconscious mind has processed and fed into a plan of action. You will be able to identify your plan and to act on it.

Once you have listed all the positive forces that were at work during your meditation, go back through the three categories and describe the inhibiting forces, those that seemed to hinder the motion of the process. The thoughts holding you back will be fairly obvious. They appear as fears, doubts and feelings of incompetence. Self-righteous thoughts and judgments of other people are inappropriate forces, as are any thoughts that place you apart from other people and in competition with them.

Make a note of those feelings that are interfering. What parts of your body feel funny? Where do you sense a weak energy flow: your stomach, libido or sexual energy? What areas are cold: your hands, feet or head? Which parts of you feel dull and sick? What emotions and feelings do you experience with each action in your meditation?

Finally, describe any inappropriate knowledge that you have. If, for example, you devise a plan that is aimed at taking advantage of other people or winning out over others, you may want to repeat the exercise. Something has broken your circuit of self-empowerment somewhere along the line.

Transcendence

The last section of the journal deals with transcendence. This is an important concept in the applied active meditation program. In transcendence, you look for the appropriate force that is the opposite of an inappropriate force. Then you replace the negative with the positive. Transcendence is one of the most powerful tools available to you. You do not correct what is inappropriate, you *replace* it. When you replace anything inappropriate with what is appropriate, you become more powerful.

Transcendence is developing within yourself the power and wisdom to replace whatever in your life is undesirable and inappropriate with that which is exciting, desirable and appropriate. Through transcendence, almost every problem in your life becomes an opportunity to increase your own personal power.

It sometimes seems the reason life has so many problems is to give us multiple chances to expand and evolve. Every time you transcend a problem rather than merely solving it, you increase awareness.

For example, suppose someone takes an unfair business advantage of you. You can become angry, try to fight back and hurt the individual. And even if you win—what do you win? Instead you can transcend this situation. You can set up a business plan that will increase your personal wealth by far more than you lost.

Or you can write a love letter or note and set up a wonderful dinner with a person you care about. Or you can add to your knowledge in a way that builds your abilities and powers. In each instance, by transcending the situation rather than reacting to it, you have gained resources you did not previously have.

What is the difference between solving problems and transcending them? Solving problems is a function of the conscious mind. To rectify a problem, you must concentrate on it. And by concentrating and putting it in the forefront of your mind, you are likely to attract more of the same. If you solve the problem, you are the same person who had that problem to begin with. You have not evolved or changed. When the problem recurs—as it most likely will—you will know the solution, and you can apply it. But you are stuck.

Almost all our education has trained us to focus on and identify with our problems, virtually assuring that we will spend our life solving the same problems over and over and over again. To step off this treadmill, remember that any problem we face is the direct result of the specific forces that produced it. Identifying the forces that are influencing us is a function of our total mind: conscious, subconscious and paraconscious.

In transcendence, you concentrate on pulling more intelligence from the universal mind into the field of your awareness, thus expanding it. You do not focus on the particular problem. For instance, I described to you earlier the particular health problem I had—a grossly enlarged prostate gland. I learned not to focus on that problem, but rather to identify the forces that had my physical self out of balance and to concentrate on restoring the functions of my entire body. Rather than treat symptoms, we corrected causes. This process left me with a stronger and better body. It transformed me. I became more powerful and resourceful.

You can experience the same kind of growth by practicing transcendence. When you use your encounter with a problem to practice transcendence, you are not the same person afterward. You have evolved. When you apply the opposite force to the one that produced the problem, you not only solve the problem, but you also add a positive force to your energy field. This force is now yours to call on whenever you need it.

Transcendence is possible because the universe is bipolar. It is made-up of opposite energies—positive and negative. When positive and negative poles are connected by a conductor, energy flows. When warm air from the south moves northward and cold air from the north moves southward, they meet to create an incredibly strong flow of energy called the jet stream.

In your life, the joining of a negative experience with its opposite positive can also create tremendous energy. Negative experiences by themselves impede or even stop the flow of universal creative energy through you. Positive experiences by themselves improve your energy flow somewhat. But the greatest power of all comes from joined polarities. A life restricted to positive experiences will be a less radiant life than one in which positive and negative are joined. Every time you connect a negative experience to a positive one and turn on the "current" by taking action, you create within yourself an enormous flow of creative energy.

The key point is that a negative experience remains negative only as long as it is not joined to a positive experience. Thus the loss of function and the resultant miseries arising from negative experiences are not from the experiences themselves. Rather, they emanate from the failure to link those negative experiences to matching positives. And in every new linkage you achieve the potential to create enormous new powers within you. That is transcendence—taking individual negative experiences, linking them to positive experiences, and creating within your body, mind and soul new and greater power than ever existed before.

Your journal is the perfect place to apply the principle of transcendence. You have been writing about the inappropriate forces at work on you. You can then concentrate on applying their opposites. You have then described the forces operating at every level of your mind. At the conscious level, the thinking level, you can concentrate on the appropriate thoughts at work during your meditation. At the subconscious level, focus on the appropriate feelings. And at the paraconscious level, concentrate on the appropriate knowing.

Discovering the Direction of Your Life

To complete the meditation, you must take the action suggested to you by the universal mind. Use your journal to describe this action in detail. Was it spontaneous? How immediate was it? As a result of the action, what do you now know?

Each entry will be a record of the circuit of self-empowerment. Your journal makes you active in the flow of your life. You can read it and see yourself unfold. The essence of your life lies not in the things happening to you, but in the relationship you establish between the universal mind and those events. As you enlarge your awareness and broaden your perspective, you will establish a closer relationship between the universal mind and what goes on in your daily life. You will discover abilities you didn't know you had, and be brought face to face with the meaning of your existence. You will discover your life has, indeed, been going somewhere—however blind you have been to its direction.

No matter how much success you achieve through the methods described in this book, you can always achieve more. I don't use the word "success" in its conventional meaning. I'm not talking about competing and winning or about amassing material possessions only. I'm talking about completing a meditation and coming out of it with another bit of intelligence from the universal mind added to your life. Success in these terms is never a stopping place. The journey doesn't end. You will not collect more of the same material goods. Rather, you will achieve your desires and discover enticing opportunities for greater personal growth. You will continually achieve new heights, the scaling of one peak taking you to view another, higher one.

Through your journal, each circuit of self-empowerment you complete and experience opens new and greater possibilities for you. It sets the stage for your next, even more transformational circuit of self-empowerment. Your life becomes a constant flow.

The purpose of your temporary physical life is to bring as much intelligence from the universal mind to your eternal self as you can.

Applied active meditation achieves its results by multiplying the effects of your circuits of self-empowerment. The impact is cumulative. Each time you use the process, its momentum increases. It will soon become autonomous—self-generating and self-directing. Through applied active meditation and the use of your journal, you continually grow. You move closer to being one with the universal mind, the force that created you. You become the co-creator of your life. And your life becomes bliss.

3
BREATHING TO ALTER STATES OF CONSCIOUSNESS

> If the Sun and Moon should doubt,
> They'd immediately go out.
> —William Blake, "Auguries of Innocence"

The efficiency of our physical, mental, emotional and spiritual functions are enhanced or weakened by the manner in which we breathe. All of the processes done in this book will be greatly improved by effective breathing. It's a *must* for maximum results.

Your life is dependent on breathing. You can exist for some time without eating, and for a shorter time without drinking, but not much longer than seven minutes without breathing. Breathing affects your vitality and health. It plays a major role in realigning mind and body. It can help you do away with fear, worry, stress and most emotional problems. Effective breathing can help unfold the latent powers within you. If you do not breathe right, no matter how diligent you are otherwise in implementing the processes presented here, your increase in personal power will be limited.

I'm going to use this chapter to teach you how to breathe effectively. As you do the exercises, you might want to begin writing in your journal what you are experiencing.

The Six Levels of Breathing

The six different levels of breathing are:

1. High breathing, or clavicular
2. Mid-breathing, or intercostal

31

3. Low breathing, or diaphragmatic
4. The complete breath
5. Full breathing, or pelvic
6. Correct breathing, or paradoxical

Level 1—High Breathing

High breathing is called clavicular because when you breathe this way, you raise your clavicle, or collarbone, in short, abrupt movements. This very fast, shallow breathing expands your lungs hardly at all, filling the top part only—to about one-eighth capacity. High breathing typically occurs when you are in a panic. Since your lungs are not filled, your blood does not get enough oxygen to distribute throughout your body. You can feel weak and paralyzed.

Your brain uses twenty percent of the oxygen in your blood. When you panic, you have difficulty thinking clearly. High breathing under any conditions interferes with your flow of thoughts. It causes thought paralysis because not enough oxygen is getting to the brain.

When the brain gets enough oxygen and sugar, which are its nutrients, it strengthens and activates the hippocampus, the area of the brain that activates the five physical senses. What the senses perceive then goes to the part of the brain called the thalamus, which edits out information not pertaining to the particular state you are in. The rest is sent to the pituitary gland. The pituitary gland then synthesizes this information, and based on what it says, activates all of the glands of your endocrine system, including the adrenal glands, which in turn activate your gonadal system. The gonadal system is the energy source for your entire body. It activates the pancreas and the liver. Your liver produces sugar that is immediately regulated by insulin from your pancreas. That sugar supplies your whole body with strength and energy.

The whole physiological process depends upon having that main fuel, oxygen, come to the brain. Therefore, the more you fill your lungs, the better off you are. A brain that is operating with very little oxygen produces a high frequency of beta brain waves, with low amplitude. This means that the brain has little capacity for radiating energy.

Level 2—Mid-Breathing

Mid-breathing is also called intercostal because it expands the chest and ribs. The muscles in between the ribs are the intercostal muscles. If you use the middle portion of your rib cage to breathe, you can expand your lungs more fully—to approximately twenty-five percent capacity. While mid-breathing also produces beta brain waves, it's more effective than high breathing. It provides enough oxygen to keep body and brain functioning, but at low levels.

Mid-breathing is the predominant pattern in Western civilization. It is the kind of breathing that encourages submission to outside authority.

Level 3—Low Breathing

Low breathing originates in the diaphragm, a partition of muscles and tendons between the chest and abdominal cavities. With diaphragmatic breathing, the lungs are five-eighths full, and the brain predominantly functions in alpha.

As you will recall, the alpha brain wave is associated with the subconscious part of the mind that regulates all bodily functions. With low breathing, your subconscious mind works the way it should, automatically regulating physiological functions. With high or mid-breathing, the subconscious mind does not function the way it should. Your body gets out of balance.

Learning to breathe from the diaphragm is the first step to correct breathing. Take a moment to feel how your body moves when you breathe from your diaphragm. When you inhale, your abdomen will expand and your lower ribs lift. Your chest will remain stationary. Place one hand on your abdomen and the other hand on your chest. Now inhale. If you are using your diaphragm, the hand on your abdomen should move out while the hand on your chest does not move. Practice this until you can do it with ease.

By breathing from your diaphragm, you pull the air down into the lungs. The farther down your diaphragm moves, the more your lungs fill with air. Once you can breathe this way easily, you can begin to develop a rhythm. Inhale for a count of 8. (Each count is approximately one second.) Hold your breath for a count of 8. Exhale for a count of 8. Hold out for a count of 4. Repeat the sequence: Inhale for 8, hold for 8, exhale for 8 and hold for 4. With rhythmic, diaphragmatic breathing, you are beginning to train your body to become aware of and establish effective breathing patterns.

Level 4—The Complete Breath

Once diaphragmatic breathing becomes natural for you, you are ready to progress to the fourth level, which is called the complete breath. The complete breath begins with the diaphragm. Inhale as you do when practicing low breathing. Once you have completed the inhale, move your breath up to fill the middle part of your lungs, pushing out your lower ribs, breastbone and chest. You will feel pressure around your ribs as you do this. Keep the breath moving and fill the top of your lungs. You upper chest will expand and your upper ribs lift. Your abdomen will be slightly drawn in to support your filling lungs.

Try placing your hands on your abdomen and chest so you can feel the movement of each part of your body. Your abdomen expands on the inhale. Then your chest begins to enlarge as you move the air up to the top of your lungs.

Now exhale slowly, letting your breath out much more slowly than you took it in. In all these breathing exercises, you will discover that the slower the exhalation, the greater its power. As you exhale, hold your chest in a firm position and draw your abdomen in a little, slowly lifting it upwards as the air leaves your lungs. When the air is exhaled, relax your chest and abdomen. With a little practice, the complete breath will become almost automatic.

With the complete breath, all parts of your respiratory system are exercised. It combines the low, middle and high breaths, moving rapidly from one level to the next forming one continuous breath. The complete breath has an alpha rhythm and works to keep the subconscious mind on track.

Level 5—Full Breathing

Once you've mastered the complete breath technique, your breathing can be stretched to an even greater level of effectiveness through practice of the full breath, or the pelvic breath. At this level of breathing, instead of just lifting your lower ribs, you draw your diaphragm even deeper. When you inhale, your whole pelvis expands—not just the abdominal portion. Begin by drawing your diaphragm down. Keep doing so until you feel your pelvis beginning to extend. Then go into the rest of the stages of the complete breath: move the air up into your lungs, feeling your chest expand.

The full breath fills your lungs nearly completely and supplies maximum oxygen to your brain. Through it, you activate your whole lower intestinal area, which is your gonadic or generative system, the energy source for your entire body. It is your butane tank; the oxygen is your pilot light. When you inhale, you inspire. One meaning of the word inspire is to set on fire. And the oxygen in the gonadic system sets your entire generative energy on fire.

Most diseases first show their signs in the abdominal area. But the brain is the place where disease actually starts. The brain without sufficient oxygen and energy loses its capacity to regulate body function. Full breathing keeps the generative process and its energy flowing. It also keeps the flow even, so you don't go from tremendous energy highs to devastating lows.

Level 6—Correct Breathing

The sixth level of breathing, the most powerful of all, is the so-called paradoxical or reverse breathing. The Tibetan masters of breathing call this correct breathing. Some of you will find it unnatural. If it requires conscious effort, produces tension and does not become automatic, don't use it.

In diaphragmatic breathing, your abdomen extends as you inhale. In paradoxical breathing, your abdomen pulls inward as you inhale. You will feel the air moving strongly throughout your entire pelvic area. You may experience the feel of oxygen entering your gonadic system.

When you inhale paradoxically, there will be a hollow point in your abdomen. The Tibetans train themselves so they can walk around with a football in the hollow of their abdomen. The football stays put as long as they don't exhale. The moment they exhale, the belly plunges back, and out pops the ball—with a lot of power.

The training that paradoxical breathing requires gives you great control over your intestinal area and gonadic system. If this level of breathing seems to be too difficult for you, do not despair. Most of us have had no experience at all in this kind of breathing. Knowing that it is a possibility may be enough. Practicing it from time to time may also suffice.

For you to make progress in this book, the most important level of breathing is level four, the complete breath. Be sure you have mastered it before you proceed to the breathing rhythms that follow. The complete breath combines the first three levels of breathing and fills your lungs. Whether you inhale by pushing your diaphragm down and extending your abdomen (low breathing), by thrusting your pelvis out (full breathing) or by collapsing your abdomen (paradoxical breathing), you must fill your lungs to the top before you begin to exhale. Once you can do this, you will be receptive to the rest of the exercises in this book.

Breathing Rhythms
and States of Consciousness

Aside from these different *levels* of breathing, there are different *rhythms* of breathing. You practiced one rhythm—8, 8, 8, 4—when you first tried breathing from the diaphragm. The important thing about rhythms is they are directly linked to different levels of consciousness. Ground breaking experiments on Jack Schwarz at the Menninger Clinic and the Langley Porter Neuropsychiatric Institute demonstrated this.

For a long time Jack has had the ability to produce different brain wave states—beta, alpha, delta or theta—on command. He knows what each different state feels like, and he can duplicate that feeling whenever he chooses. Before the experiments, he did not know exactly how he moved from state to state. Researchers wanted to figure out the mechanics behind his amazing ability. They used sophisticated instruments to measure Jack's physiological processes as he changed from one state to another. After many measurements, scientists found only one variable as Jack moved from one brain wave state to the next: his breathing rhythm. Whenever he was asked to go to a different brain wave frequency, Jack changed the pattern of his breathing.

Researchers at the Menninger Foundation recorded his breathing rhythms and then tested a large number of people, asking them to breathe as he had. In every case, a specific breathing rhythm produced the same brain wave activity. This pioneering research is extremely exciting because it means all of us can move into any state of consciousness we desire if we know the breathing rhythm associated with that state!

In the rest of this chapter, I'm going to describe these breathing rhythms for you. In the exercises, you will consciously move yourself into specific brain wave states by altering the rhythm of your breathing. The purpose of these exercises is to show you what each brain wave state *feels like*. Once you know the feeling, then you'll be able to move into that state whenever you wish.

Use these exercises to increase your awareness of how you breathe during various circumstances in your life. If a certain rhythm is not helpful in a particular situation, you have the power to change it. After you concentrate on your breathing rhythms for a time, your subconscious mind will take control and automatically change the rhythm to put you into the most appropriate state for whatever situation you're in.

Breathing Exercises

In the breathing pattern exercises you are about to do, again I advise using your journal to keep track of what happens. Write down what you experience physically and emotionally in each state of consciousness. The goal of the exercises is to become aware of what each state feels like to you.

In these exercises you will be given counts. For example, inhale for a count of 8. Each count is approximately one second. So inhaling for a count of 8 is inhaling for approximately eight seconds.

To be effective, your breathing must be either diaphragmatic or pelvic. Before beginning the exercises, be sure you can easily breathe diaphragmatically and/or pelvically. To get maximum oxygen to the brain, inhale through both nostrils and exhale through the mouth or nostrils, whichever feels correct to you.

To warm up for the start of the exercises, practice breathing rhythmically. Breathe in for a count of 8. Hold the breath in for the same count. Exhale for the same count. Then wait for a count of four. Repeat: Inhale for 8, hold for 8, exhale for 8, wait for 4.

Once you can comfortably breathe diaphragmatically and/or pelvically and rhythmically you are ready to begin your exercises. You must learn to do these patterns not only sitting comfortably at home, but at all times and in all situations during your daily life.

Beta Breathing

Beta breathing is the breathing most people do all day long. When you are not concentrating on your breathing, you tend to breathe at the clavicular or intercostal level. It is very important, however, in *all* of the exercises that you use only the diaphragmatic or pelvic full breath. You never use clavicular or intercostal breathing in any exercise. This will not give you the oxygen you need for awareness. The point of the exercise is to become acquainted with the rhythm of beta breathing, which is 4, 4, 4, 4. Concentrate on the way this rhythm feels.

Begin now. Always use the diaphragmatic or pelvic complete breath.

Inhale for four seconds: 1, 2, 3, 4.
Hold in the breath for four seconds: 1, 2, 3, 4.
Exhale for four seconds: 1, 2, 3, 4.
Wait for four seconds: 1, 2, 3, 4.

By breathing in the beta rhythm, you concentrate your energy in the conscious function of your mind. No matter how deep your breathing, if the rhythm is 4, 4, 4, 4, the conscious mind will be predominant.

Alpha Breathing

Alpha brain waves are associated with the functioning of your subconscious mind. Thus when alpha waves are dominant, you are mainly using your subconscious mind. As we have discussed, the subconscious mind regulates your body functions and stores all your experiences. It relates all that is happening to you in the present to your past experiences. Pain control takes place in the alpha state. When you are in alpha, you will feel relaxed without feeling drowsy.

The pattern for alpha is 8, 8, 8, 4.
To practice the alpha rhythm, inhale for eight seconds: 1, 2, 3,
    4, 5, 6, 7, 8.
Hold in the breath: 1, 2, 3, 4, 5, 6, 7, 8. Exhale: 1, 2, 3, 4, 5, 6,
    7, 8.
Wait: 1, 2, 3, 4.

The waiting count helps to keep your rhythm even. If you find you need oxygen after you have exhaled—if you can't wait comfortably for 4 counts—you had better look to restoring your whole breathing pattern. Make sure you are doing complete breathing. Waiting only four seconds should be effortless.

The Alpha-Theta Transfer

The key to your ability to change brain wave states at will is recognition of what the different states feel like. At this point in your development of breathing rhythms, an intermediate step—the transfer from alpha to theta—will help you increase your awareness of the differences in the two states. It also introduces a more effective inhale, one that you will always use to change your state of consciousness to the paraconscious.

The alpha-theta transfer pattern is 4, 8, 8, 4.

The 8 count in the previous exercise was a mild inhalation. Now the inhalation is to a 4 count. This is a faster and more vigorous inhalation. You have to get the same amount of oxygen in a 4 count that you previously did in an 8 count.

Breathe in from the diaphragm or pelvis: 1, 2, 3, 4.
Hold in the breath: 1, 2, 3, 4, 5, 6, 7, 8.
Exhale: 1, 2, 3, 4, 5, 6, 7, 8.
Wait: 1, 2, 3, 4.

Once you are comfortable with this pattern, you can move to the next exercise.

Theta Breathing

Theta brain waves are associated with the paraconscious mind. When you are predominately in theta, you are going from your physical ego, your I self, into relations with your non-physical, eternal self. Thus in theta you are bringing into your mind information, intelligence and happenings that you cannot experience in the material world. This is the first level of connection that you make with the non-physical universe surrounding you and out of which you are created. It is also the first connection you make with your eternal self.

The theta pattern is 4, 8, 16, 4.

Note it is the exhalation that is changed. You will be exhaling for a longer count than in the previous exercise. Try it.

Breathe in from the diaphragm or pelvis: 1, 2, 3, 4.
Hold in: 1, 2, 3, 4, 5, 6, 7, 8.
Exhale: 1, 2, 3, 4, 5, 6, 7, 8, 9, 10, 11, 12, 13, 14, 15, 16.
Wait: 1, 2, 3, 4.

Keep breathing in the theta rhythm until you can comfortably do it. Notice how you feel when your breath moves this way. Be sure you are thoroughly familiar with the theta state before you move on to the next level.

Delta Breathing

Delta brain waves put you into the deepest possible contact with subtle universal energies. When in your waking daily life you use delta brain waves, you will receive information about the nature of the universe, about infinity itself.

The delta pattern is 4, 8, 32, 4.

Once again, the change is in the length of your exhalation. At this level, you need to be careful not to let too much breath out too early.

Breathe in vigorously from the diaphragm or pelvis: 1, 2, 3, 4.
Hold in: 1, 2, 3, 4, 5, 6, 7, 8.
Exhale: 1, 2, 3, 4, 5, 6, 7, 8, 9, 10, 11, 12, 13, 14, 15, 16, 17, 18,
    19, 20, 21, 22, 23, 24, 25, 26, 27, 28, 29, 30, 31, 32.
Wait: 1, 2, 3, 4.

For those of you who ran out of breath before 32, 1 have an analogy that might help. Compare your exhalation to a trip through a desert. The desert stretches from point A to point B. I'm going to be your guide on this trip, and I advise you to take along a bottle of water. The water has to last from point A to point B. Don't gulp it. When you feel thirsty, just wet your lips and distribute the water very carefully. If you do this, you will arrive at point B without thirst and even with some water left in the bottle.

Try the delta pattern again, being more careful this time with the amount of breath you expend as you exhale. Practice until delta breathing is comfortable for you.

A Combination Exercise

Once you are familiar with each of the separate states, you are ready for the final exercise, which is to integrate them all. Take your time and go carefully through this exercise, noting the changes in the way you feel as you move from alpha to theta to delta.

First, do three alpha rhythms: 8, 8, 8, 4.
Next, do three alpha-theta transfers: 4, 8, 8, 4.
Be aware of how the transfer feels.
Now do two alpha rhythms (8, 8, 8, 4) and one theta (4, 8, 16, 4).
How does each feel to you?
Make notes in your journal.
Finally, you are ready to go all the way into delta. Do two alpha rhythms (8, 8, 8, 4), one theta (4, 8, 16, 4) and one delta (4, 8, 32, 4).

The Body During Theta and Delta

When you go into the paraconscious theta and delta states, your physiological functions are on automatic pilot. Your body remains perfectly regulated while you explore deeper levels of the universal mind.

Think of the physiological functions of your body as an engine. The alpha state is the fuel that runs this engine. The engine is located in the corpus callosum area of the brain. Jack Schwarz's studies have discovered that the moment a person dives into theta, both hemispheres of the brain start to operate in a very balanced way. But the corpus callosum remains in alpha and continues to regulate our body functions. Strong alpha waves have been measured in the corpus callosum when the predominant brain wave state is theta or delta.

On automatic pilot, your body functions on its own. You can turn all your attention toward the information coming in through your theta or delta level.

Breathing and Repression of Feelings

As you learn the steps toward applied active meditation, you will discover the value of effective breathing. In the next chapter, when you go through the cosmic review, you will begin building a model to test the validity of all that you are doing in this book. For now, however, I want you to consider using these breathing techniques to help you express your emotions more fully.

In my experience, a major, if not *the* major cause of physical, mental and emotional malfunctions is *repressed emotion*. Emotion is energy in motion. When emotions are repressed, the flow of energy is stopped. When you repress your emotions, you prevent your energy from being expressed. When energy flow is blocked, your body and your self malfunction. You experience an increase in tension. You tire easily and often feel frustrated.

Through breathing, you set energy free. Particularly when you are in the higher states of consciousness, your subconscious mind regulates all the physiological functions of your body to their maximum. As a result, you increase the energy flow to every activity of your life. You'll find that when you are continuously breathing effectively, you will be more expressive. As you go into theta and delta states, you won't hold back as much. You will express more. And you will find yourself more in balance.

The Right Breathing Pattern for You

Different situations require different breathing patterns. You can apply a simple test to determine whether you are breathing in a way beneficial to you. If you feel increasingly relaxed and at ease, you are using the proper pattern. For instance, you might be driving your car when someone pulls out in front of you. You have to swerve to avoid hitting the other car. You immediately feel anger, one of the energy-blocking emotions. You want to choose a breathing pattern that will release anger and tension and let energy flow easily through you.

For a time—it took me six months—you will have to consciously choose different breathing patterns and experiment with them. You are looking for the pattern that gives you the greatest energy flow and adds the most to your strength and power. You want to feel the greatest relaxation. As your relaxation increases, so will your excitement! After awhile, your subconscious mind will take control of your breathing and automatically produce the pattern that's best for each situation.

The Excitement Factor

Using your breathing to produce specific brain waves and to move from one state of consciousness to another will have little benefit if the amplitude or voltage of the brain waves you are producing is low. With low power, changing brain wave frequency is meaningless. High power must accompany whatever brain wave frequency you choose for that frequency to be effective for you and to transfer to you the information and understanding you need to achieve whatever you desire.

Excitement is the greatest source of power available to you. Please take the word excitement literally. By definition, to excite is to call to activity and to energize. And this is exactly what excitement does to your brain waves—it increases their activity and amplitude.

A high level of excitement also stirs up the chemistry in your body so it can set free energy that has been trapped. Your body is made-up of molecules. These molecules are bundles of bound-together atoms. The binding force is energy. More specifically, the binding force is the energy relinquished by ions, which are atoms that have an electrical charge. Ions fuse together to form molecules. In the fusion, the electrical charge of the ions is given over to the holding together of the molecule. Thus every molecule in your body is filled with energy waiting to be released. We know from splitting the atom how much trapped energy there is to be released.

The power you produce and radiate is the direct consequence of the energy you allow to enter your body and move freely within it. High energy production makes you almost immune to both disease and failure! Obviously it is of basic and extreme importance to understand what you can do to free your energy and what you do that keeps it trapped.

A major cause of imprisoned energy is questioning thinking. Will they like me or not? Will I be accepted or not? What if? Will this work out as I want it to, or will I fail? Am I smart enough to do this? Do I have the ability to succeed in this or not? Am I good enough? What fears do I have? Fears imprison and stop the flow of almost all energy. According to the famous positive thinker Napoleon Hill, the six basic fears are, in descending order of importance: poverty, criticism, ill health, lost love, old age and death.

Every book that purports to be a recipe for success will have one main ingredient—positive thinking. Every course on how to get rich, how to improve your health, how to find true love will exhort you to increase your excitement level and decrease your fears and doubts. To do this, you must have desire, faith, high expectations and the ability to use your total mind. The combination of these ingredients will send your voltage sky high. You will then operate at a high level of power.

Another element you need to understand in this whole issue of excitement is spontaneity. When your excitement is high, you act spontaneously. You do not allow doubt to enter your mind. You do not allow fears to paralyze you. When you act immediately and spontaneously, you will feel the flow of energy. Don't be afraid. Don't worry about having to conserve your energy. You can remain at a high level of excitement indefinitely!

Excitement brings great energy into your body. It breaks open those molecules and liberates the energy from them. With each breath you take, feel the increase in your powers, feel the level of your personal radiation rising.

You are creating a circuit, using your excitement and breath to make a divine connection. You will feel universal power and intelligence flow through you. Your excitement level cannot help but increase as you become aware of this flow and know it is continuous and cumulative. You are adding intelligence from the universal mind to your temporal self and to your eternal self, and you are helping the evolution of the universe itself to proceed. This is your circuit of transcendence. It is the bottom line of the process called life. Nothing could be more exciting.

4

THE COSMIC REVIEW

> *If the doors of perception were cleansed everything*
> *would appear as it is, infinite.*
> —William Blake, "A Memorable Fancy"

The techniques of applied active meditation that you are learning through this book are unique. They give you the ability to obtain the greatest possible powers for yourself. The techniques are practical. You do not sit in a corner and meditate for an hour or two. The meditation is done *all day* every day. It is an active meditation that you put into daily use. The techniques are designed to become an integral part of your life.

There are six segments to applied active meditation. The basic purpose is the same for each segment, namely to add intelligence from the universal mind to your daily life. However, each segment is applied differently, with different focuses and specific purposes. The segments can be used together, separately or in any conceivable combination. The six segments of the applied active meditation are:

1. *The Cosmic Review*—Its purpose is to review past actions and add intelligence from the universal mind to them. Every time you do this, you permanently increase your own personal power, making your life a continual growth process. You are on the circuit of self-empowerment.

2. *Psycho-physical Rehearsal, Part One*—This process adds intelligence from the universal mind to what you are experiencing at this very moment. It immediately increases

your power to respond to whatever is occurring this instant in your life.

3. *Psycho-physical Rehearsal, Part Two*—This process adds intelligence from the universal mind to future events in your life. If you know of an event coming up, you prepare for it by rehearsing it in such a way as to add intelligence from the universal mind to it. When the event arrives, you are in a position of great power and insight because of this preparation.

4. *Autogenic Psycho-physical Rehearsal*—The autogenic psycho-physical rehearsal is one in which you yourself generate the subject for the psycho-physical rehearsal. This process integrates the first three levels of applied active meditation. The cosmic review and parts one and two of the psycho-physical rehearsal all focus on one particular time frame: past, present or future. The autogenic psycho-physical rehearsal applies to all levels of your life and being. It is a segment of meditation you can practice while you are doing routine tasks or in contemplation of the commonplace.

5. *The Guided Meditation*—This process enables you to discover a theme of prime meaning to you. In the guided meditation, you use a script or story from your conscious mind as something on which to focus. Because you are trying to discover a theme, you will direct the way this meditation goes. You will consciously alter the scene to add any emotions you wish to observe or actions you wish to experience. As you proceed, your paraconscious mind will let you know which themes or ideas are most important.

6. *The Creative Meditation*—This process explores the theme that was presented to you during the guided meditation. It can also be used with any other theme important to you. In contrast to the guided meditation, it is almost completely controlled by the paraconscious function of your mind. It is free-flowing and brings you into the widest possible contact with the universal mind. Enlightenment—the deepest possible entry into the universal mind—is the objective.

The cosmic review is the first piece of applied active meditation. It's the initial step in developing your ability to use your total mind to transform intelligence from the universal mind into personal power. By conducting the cosmic review, you will begin to use your paraconscious mind and to apply its insights to your daily life.

Until now you have been using, at most, only two-thirds of your mind. No matter how much you have achieved, you are still failing to live up to your potential. No matter how rich you have become, you are still dwelling in poverty. To live abundantly, you must begin to use the third part of your mind: the paraconscious.

Abundance is not something you achieve, or get, or have. Abundance is a process. Abundance is the process of transforming intelligence and power from the universal mind into personal intelligence and power. It is a continuous, never-ending process. Each successful transformation forms the foundation for the next, even more powerful transformation.

To transform power from the universal mind into personal power, your paraconscious mind contacts the universal mind and directs its intelligence to your subconscious. This new input mixes with the information stored in the subconscious mind. It stirs up the contents and adds great power and insight. This additional power is reflected in the plans the subconscious mind sends to the conscious mind. And the actions the conscious mind directs will have a new potency.

As mentioned in the last chapter, the conscious mind must spontaneously direct the actions suggested by the subconscious mind. If the conscious mind stops to think, to doubt or to raise fears, the process is broken. The flow of the intelligence from the universal mind stops, and its power is lost to you. Taking spontaneous action is tremendously important.

Taking action completes one circuit of self-empowerment. Only after you take the suggested action is the newest acquisition of intelligence from the universal mind permanently registered in your subconscious mind. Only after an action does this addition of intelligence from the universal mind become a power that will be available to you for the rest of your life.

The Law of Equivalent Returns

With each addition of power, the likelihood of attracting more power increases. This is the universal law of harmony in action. The law of harmony says that in the non-material world, the eternal world, like attracts like. In the material world unlike poles attract each other. So thoughts, which are non-material, attract similar thoughts and lead to actions that are in harmony with them.

A particular part of the law of harmony is the law of equivalent returns. This says that whatever you concentrate on and focus your attention on, you are in harmony with, and you will achieve. If you concentrate and focus on success, that is what you will achieve. If you concentrate and focus on what you fear, that is what you will attract.

The major reason there is so much misery and failure in the world is that the majority of people spend their lives concentrating on problems. And the problems we face have increased. The law of equivalent returns tells why. We achieve whatever we concentrate on. If the focus is on problems, we will have more problems—even if we appear to solve an immediate difficulty.

For example, when we concentrate on fighting crime, as our present history dramatically shows, the result is we have more crime. When we fight diseases, as today's staggering medical bills and mounting suffering confirm, we have more diseases. All this is predictable by the law of universal harmony and its equivalent returns.

If, instead of concentrating on problems or on what is wrong in their lives, people would concentrate on what they want, what they wish to achieve, they would make progress. For example, when people are economically down and out, if they concentrated on abundance instead of on lack, they would achieve abundance. If, instead of concentrating on defeating racism, we concentrated on achieving brotherhood, there would be a dramatic drop in bigotry. If, rather than focusing on fighting crime and building costly jails, we stressed harmony and mutual assistance, we would have little crime. If, instead of combating drugs, we put our efforts into encouraging lives of joy and quality, the drug problem would disappear. If, instead of battling disease, we concentrated on health, the incidence of disease would dramatically decrease.

The law of equivalent returns tells why a positive mental attitude is so powerful—and a negative one so destructive. With a positive mental attitude, your brain focuses on and chooses positive stimuli and ideas. You seem to attract success. In reality, you are choosing success. When your conscious-subconscious mind believes that only success will come your way, then from the barrage of stimuli it selects those that will result in your success.

Since your brain chooses to acknowledge predominantly those stimuli that reinforce your belief systems, what you believe is of crucial importance. And even more crucial is the degree to which you believe. In other words, your mind must be totally filled with whatever you want to attract or you will probably not realize your goals. Even a few fears or doubts remaining in your mind can block the achievement of your desires.

As a human being, you have the freedom to place into your mind whatever you choose. Once you have installed a belief system, however, your freedom is severely restricted. The conscious mind will act according to the resident belief system. The beliefs lodged in your mind determine what you will perceive and what actions you will take.

What the Cosmic Review Can Do

Virtually all of us encounter problems and frustrations. Sometimes we suffer severely. We have been taught to look at problems as undesirable and even horrible. However, as you will experience with the cosmic review, through your problems you can achieve a higher state. You can use them to establish circuits of self-empowerment and hence to increase your personal power and energy.

The cosmic review is a specific process for going over problems, then using your total mind power to transcend them. I explained the difference between problem solving and transcending in Chapter 2. It is critical that you understand this difference.

Almost every negative experience offers you the opportunity to connect to a positive and by so doing to increase your personal power. When you link the negatives of the pain and suffering of your daily life to the positives of success and happiness brought to you from the universal mind, you create an energy within you that gives you the insight and power to achieve more success and happiness than you could have achieved without this linkage. Once you complete the circuit of self-empowerment, the additional power is yours to use for the rest of your life.

The concept of transcendence has three important parts. First, you must understand the significance and potential of all experiences. Second, you must find a way to join earthly negative experience to its opposite positive in the universal mind. The most effective process for doing this is meditation. Third, you must express the action suggested by the universal mind in your daily life. It is the expression of the positive action from the universal mind that allows your life current to flow.

Through the cosmic review, you can take several important first steps toward transcendence and total mind power:

1. *You can get to know your present self.* The cosmic review will show you both the powers and the negative energy you currently possess. Once you are aware of these, you can decide which present powers to strengthen and which new ones to pursue. You can also rid yourself of the fears and negative thoughts holding you back.

2. *You can learn to use your paraconscious mind to tune into the universal mind and bring it to your **self**.* Once you put input from the paraconscious to work in your life, you will have the

key to transforming universal power into personal power, and you will be on your way to achieving everything you want.

You Are the Expert

The first time you undertake the cosmic review, I suggest you follow precisely the directions I'm about to give you. This will give you a solid point of departure. The second time you try a cosmic review, do whatever you like to make the process your own. The idea of this book is not for you to slavishly imitate my experience. You may not react the way I do to certain exercises. If you have a different reaction, go with it. If I say I experienced A, but you experience Z, then Z is the right reaction for you. Always respond the way your uniqueness requires. As you observe yourself, learn to tailor the process to your needs, desires and abilities.

Adapting processes and methods to your own needs is harder than you realize. It takes courage and responsibility. You have been conditioned to rely on experts for most of what you do in your life. This need for outside authority is deeply rooted in your conscious mind. The first step in preparing for self-awareness is to loosen the rigid control this programming exerts. Look to your teachers and experts only for guidance. Look within *yourself* for the power to achieve.

As you progress through the cosmic review, become aware of yourself. Pause to ask these questions at each experience: What do I think? What do I feel? What have I learned? What do I now know? Become aware of your emotions. Of your existing belief systems. Of your desires and fears. Become aware of any feelings and sensations in your body. Record the process in your journal. With the cosmic review, you will get to know your inner self as well as you know your face in the mirror.

THE STEPS OF THE COSMIC REVIEW
Creating Your Horizon

Before you try your first cosmic review, read through the instructions once for understanding. The first time you do the cosmic review follow the instructions step by step.

Begin the cosmic review *by sitting or lying down*. Be sure you feel relaxed. With as little tension in your body as possible. Breathe deeply and steadily. Move into a theta or a delta rhythm. Or use the breathing pattern that feels best to you, the one that puts you at ease and produces maximum relaxation.

Once you are relaxed, *close your eyes* and concentrate only on what you are creating. First, *mentally create a horizon*. Once the horizon is there, *create a field* leading to it. *Paint the field* in whatever colors you like. My field is a beautiful green. Yours may be a field of golden wheat. Or a field of wild flowers. Do not force yourself to create a green field. Whatever color you see is what your paraconscious is letting you know is correct for you. Whatever color, experience it and the horizon it leads to. Beyond the horizon, *create a sky*. The sky may be a pale blue, or darkness. Whatever sky you see is the one your paraconscious has picked as right for you. My sky is a light blue.

On the horizon *add a movie screen*. When I try to paint a movie screen on my horizon, I create instead a very light-colored half sun. I prefer that to the screen. Most people prefer a movie screen. Place whatever your paraconscious mind tells you to on your horizon. The idea is to create a surface on which you can watch scenes from your life. A movie screen works very well for this. But if your paraconscious mind tells you to put a boat with a huge white sail on your horizon, don't hesitate to comply. (I will write the rest of these instructions with the assumption you are seeing a movie screen on your horizon.)

Now, *create an image of yourself*. This image can look exactly the way you do now. Or it can be a younger you. Or it can be a figure that represents you. For me, the image of myself is a stick figure. This image that you are introducing must be free of preconceived notions. It should not be an agent of your belief systems. You already have a strong identity that acts as a filter for you, admitting anything that it agrees with and blocking out that with which it disagrees. The image that you want for the cosmic review must have complete freedom. There can be no restrictions on its actions, no belief system interfering with what it perceives. This is the image through which the paraconscious and subconscious can reveal themselves. This is the part of you that can be open to new information. If you are unable to create this kind of image of yourself, you are being held back by fears, doubts and other negative feelings that you have. Go ahead with the exercise anyway. In the exercise you will discover your inappropriate emotions and beliefs. Do not at this time add the image of yourself. You will be able to include your free-thinking representative later, as you grow beyond your old belief systems.

Once you have your representative, or second self, placed in the scene you are creating, *instruct your image to walk* across the field toward the movie screen. When I do this, the stick figure that represents me always takes a position on the left side of my horizon, to the left of the screen.

Letting the Day's Events Roll

Now that you have the scene set, you begin your cosmic review.

Use your memory to *project onto the screen on your horizon everything that has occurred during the day*. Relax and let every scene you remember roll by. Watch the scenes as you would a movie. Maybe you won't get pictures at first. Maybe you will get only sound. Or perhaps you prefer the idea of seeing your day on video tape, rather than film. Whatever method reveals itself to you, use it to *review your entire day*. This review will be edited, compacted and synthesized; but it should not be censored. You are trying for a glimpse of all that you have experienced from the moment you opened your eyes until you began the review.

Watch passively as if you are looking at someone else's life. Make sure that your second self is also watching without judging. When you learn to use your own eyes to look at yourself as you are, without expectations and preconceptions, you will be taking a huge step toward increasing your personal power. Doing this daily in the cosmic review breaks the cycle of dependence on other people's expectations and opinions and on your own restrictive belief systems. It releases you from the anxiety inherent in accepting outside goals and demands. It opens you to receive intelligence from the universal mind.

As you let your day's activities roll along like a movie, observe what seemed to go smoothly for you, what went particularly well, what disturbed you. If you feel disturbed at what you see, acknowledge the feeling. When you encounter a scene that seems difficult during the review or that causes you uneasy feelings, you must look at it again. Stop the movie, and slowly replay the action. Observe how you responded. Do not try to replay the scene differently, in a way that makes you feel better. Replay it exactly as it happened. Remain a passive observer. Pay attention to the actions of your second self. If necessary, replay the action several times. Very often you will see your second self enter into the action and direct it to a more appropriate result. Do not force this to happen, but if it does happen, let it.

When things happen without any conscious effort on your part, you know this is your paraconscious mind bringing you power and intelligence from the universal mind. *The universal mind is showing you what is now appropriate* for you. You will see on your screen a more appropriate action with a more appropriate result. Where your previous action was inadequate to achieve the result you desired, the action you now observe will achieve that result for you. On the screen before you, you have seen incoming universal energy and intelligence transformed into the action needed to achieve your desires!

Seeing universal power in action does not transform it into personal power. That transformation occurs only after experiencing the action recommended to you by the universal mind. You must *act on it in your daily life*. The next time you encounter a similar situation, apply your new knowledge and power. You must do this spontaneously. If you stop to think about it or question it, you will destroy its power to work for you. If, however, you spontaneously apply it to situations in your daily life, then universal power will be yours on a personal level.

Continue with the cosmic review, carefully observing each scene from your day. Replay the scenes that cause you to wonder about the appropriateness of your actions. You might discover that some of the actions you originally thought appropriate now appear inappropriate. Replay them until your paraconscious gives you a different response. Watch your second self acting in a way that is right for you. You may want to replay the new response a few times to get the most out of it and to rehearse for the time when you will apply it in your daily life.

Examples of Real Life Cosmic Reviews

The following are two cosmic reviews. They are situations that actually occurred in real life.

Building a Highly Successful Patient-Centered Dental Practice

A dental specialist had a successful practice. He took in one associate. After about 20 years they took in a second associate. The two associates felt they could increase their income by changing the practice in ways the senior partner could not ethically agree with. So the two junior partners asked him to leave the practice.

After they separated, the two junior partners sent a letter to every referring dentist of the senior partner implying they had to let him go for reasons of incompetence and stating no patients should be referred to him. They also made telephone calls to some referring dentists stating they had to let the senior partner go for the protection of the patients and to prevent lawsuits because he was becoming senile.

The senior partner could have become angry and fought back. Had he so reacted, however, the two ex-junior partners would have controlled and directed his actions. Instead he responded with a cosmic review. He saw his second self sitting at the desk in his private office. On the desk was a notebook. On the notebook was written, "Questions to ask patients."

Since the dentist did not consciously create this scene or write these notes, their source must have been the paraconscious function of the mind. The questions in this notebook asked the patient not about their disease, but about their wants and needs. Why did they choose this office? What did they expect to achieve? Why did they feel the treatment important? What was important to them?

From these notes the dentist gleaned something as important as treating a disease: understanding what the patient who has the disease *wants*. He began to focus more and more on the wants of the patient. He also found an essential part of any treatment was to use the disease and treatment time to help actually build the patient's self-image. He wanted each patient to leave the appointment feeling better about his or herself than when he or she entered. He dramatically expanded the patient interaction part of the practice, and he became far more successful than in his previous practice.

Had he reacted to the attacks on him, he would have spent his time fighting back. Instead he responded by turning to a higher need. His higher need was to create a patient-centered, self-fulfilling practice. To the joy of all, he succeeded.

In fact, much of what he did is summed up in a sentence from Dave Grant, " . . . the ultimate success of my life will not be judged by those who admire me for my accomplishments but by those who have seen their true beauty and worth in my eyes."

Delivering a Very Successful Talk

A person had an important meeting planned, but the other party did not show up. He could have reacted by getting angry at the inconsiderate individual, by name calling, even deciding how he could get back at and hurt the other person.

Or he could respond by looking for a higher need. He chose this approach and used the far wall of the room he was in as his horizon and screen. He sent his second self into the picture and then stopped all conscious mind input. He became an observer. He saw his second self speaking to a group of people. He remembered that the next week he had an important talk to deliver. He had a great deal of trouble trying to put this speech together with his conscious mind. In fact, all his efforts to date were failures.

He then saw a pen and note pad on his desk in front of him. His second self now stopped his speech, turned to the person, and pointed to the note pad. "Write this," the second self said to the observer. Since there was no conscious mind input, the only place this information could come from was the paraconscious mind function.

What the observer heard in his mind, and wrote down on his pad, was an outline of the subjects to be presented in his speech. The outline was close to perfect for the group he was to address. Not only were the subjects obvious, but the best sequence for their presentation was also covered. With this outline, our person went back to his conscious mind and had no trouble writing his talk. When he actually gave the talk it was a huge success.

Instead of reacting and being frustrated and angry, which accomplishes little, this person responded by using his paraconscious input to fill a higher need. By so doing he transcended his problem.

Devaluing Inappropriate Actions

A major objective of the cosmic review is to transmute negative experiences into positive ones. Through the cosmic review, you will learn to recognize that there is a positive side to almost every problem and frustration you encounter. You will transcend these problems and frustrations and discover personal powers you would not have achieved without them. Your sufferings can lead to joys. A line from Kahlil Gibran says that your joy of today is your sorrow of yesterday, unmasked. This speaks to the potential for increased power that suffering offers. *Without problems that cause you to stop and evaluate your actions, you would never contact the intelligence from the universal mind by which you grow and evolve.*

The process of the cosmic review aims you toward transcendence by helping you devalue those actions that have been impeding your progress. The moment you observe an action from your day and deem it inappropriate, you have devalued that action. You have reduced its value. You are no longer emotionally attached to it. As soon as you devalue an action, you free the energy that was attached to it. As long as you concentrate on inappropriate actions, your energy is invested in them and you cannot use it creatively. With energy attached to what is inappropriate for you, you keep repeating your mistakes. Devaluing an inappropriate action frees energy for transformation into something that will enhance your life.

Think about the negatives to which you give value and attach energy. If you concentrate on how dumb, inadequate or bad you were in certain situations, you are giving value to those qualities. You are attaching energy to them. The price you pay for tying up your energy in these negatives is tremendous. The cosmic review helps you free that energy. You do not pass negative judgment on yourself. You merely deem an action inappropriate, and you receive instructions from the universal mind for transcending that action. You free energy for use in increasing your personal power. You attach that energy to appropriate actions, and you move to a higher level of existence. Energy attached to appropriate actions is creative. It is in harmony with universal law.

If you know you've had a bad experience, use the cosmic review on it as soon afterward as possible. Use the review before the fear starts setting in and you begin to attach to it.

Your Journal

When you apply the power gained during the cosmic review, it becomes yours to use for the rest of your life. To keep that power accessible until you have a chance to use it, record the results of your cosmic review experiences in your journal.

The form presented in Chapter 2 will work well to record what happens during each cosmic review. However, if that form does not suit your purposes, ignore it and design your own way of keeping track of what you experience. The important thing is to record the thoughts and feelings you were aware of as you watched the events of a day unfold. What thoughts and actions struck you as appropriate? What ones seemed inappropriate? What new thoughts did you have once you had run through a complete cosmic review? Did you strengthen your appropriate thoughts? Did you devalue and transcend your inappropriate thoughts and actions?

Follow a similar line of questioning with your feelings. What feelings were you aware of? Did you notice any fears? Which feelings seemed appropriate, and which inappropriate? What new appropriate feelings did you have at the conclusion of your cosmic review? Did you strengthen your appropriate feelings and devalue your inappropriate feelings? Did you become aware of your blocking belief systems and your energizing belief systems?

After you have written about your thoughts and feelings during the cosmic review, you can write about the actions you viewed. What actions did you take during the day that were appropriate? What actions were inappropriate? What new actions were suggested to you by your cosmic review? Most important, how do you plan to implement your new power in your daily life?

Finally, what do you now know that you did not know prior to your cosmic review? What new insights are you aware of? As you apply your new insights and power, what results are you experiencing? Does it fit your model, does it expand your model?

A Summary of the Steps in the Cosmic Review

1. *With your conscious mind, set up a horizon.*

2. *Create a field leading to that horizon.*

3. *Create a sky beyond the horizon.*

4. *Set up a screen on the horizon.*

5. *Create a second self and send onto your horizon.* Your second self may enter into any actions that occur.

6. *Become an unattached observer*, merely watching the actions you see unfolding.

7. *On the screen, replay all the actions of the present day*, from the time you awoke to the moment you began the review.

8. *If you see* an action to which you wish to add intelligence from the universal mind, replay the action on your screen. Turn off the input from your conscious mind and let your paraconscious mind work. Any action you see that makes you feel uneasy or unhappy is one that needs replaying. Repeat it on the screen until the action that replaces it is free of doubts, questions and fears—and until you feel comfortable, confident and excited. You may also wish to replay other actions that seem appropriate. In so doing, you will determine whether input from the para-conscious mind will change them, adding intelligence from the universal mind.

9. *Once the review is complete, spontaneously put the new actions it suggested to use in your daily life.* Do not permit your conscious mind, with its doubts and fears, to interfere with or change the actions shown you by the paraconscious.

10. *These steps complete the circuit of self-empowerment.* The new power brought to you now becomes a permanent part of you. The cosmic review is your chance to create yourself anew each day. It is your first step into a continuously expanding self and a continuously expanding universe.

With each review, you will find new possibilities opening to you. You become thankful to the universe for both the good and the bad. And as you become proficient at many cosmic reviews, you will suddenly find you are flowing. You will find yourself in fast-forward. You will soon be on a path of daily miracles. Your journal will keep you apprised of this path. It will make for very exciting reading.

5
PSYCHO-PHYSICAL REHEARSAL

> *I must Create a System, or be enslaved by another Man's;*
> *I will not Reason and Compare: my business is to Create.*
>
> —William Blake, "Jerusalem"

All the aspects of applied active meditation are based on the principle that our universe and everything in it, including us, are composed of and controlled by electromagnetic radiation. This is the carrier of the universal mind and its intelligence. How we make use of this universal mind and the intelligence it contains determines how successful and rewarding our lives will be. It determines how we grow and evolve and what each one of us becomes during our lifetime. The greater the electromagnetic energy available for our use, the greater our power to achieve whatever we wish.

Every electromagnetic wave has two characteristics—it moves horizontally and vibrates vertically. They are arranged on a continuum according to how rapidly they vibrate. The type of information any wave carries depends on its length. The wavelength is determined by the number of complete cycles that occur in one second, or cycles per second (cps).

This relationship is explained by the simple equation: [frequency] x [wavelength] = the speed of light—or 186,282 miles per second. Maxwell showed that all electromagnetic waves travel at the speed of light. Therefore for any electromagnetic wave, the number of vibrations taking place each second, times the wavelength, must equal 186,282 miles. Thus the higher the frequency (cps), the shorter

57

the wavelength—and conversely—the lower the frequency, the greater the wavelength.

For example, if the frequency is 10,000 cps, then 10,000 times the wavelength is 186,282 miles. Dividing the speed of light by the frequency of 10,000 cps gives a wavelength of 18.6282 miles. At a frequency of 1,000 cps, we have a wavelength of 186.282 miles. At 1 cps, which is a delta brain wave emission, each wave is 186,282 miles long!

In our physical world waves of a certain length can carry pictures into our TV sets. Even longer ones carry sounds and words and ideas. A radio antenna attracts those waves carrying sounds, and a radio transforms them to within human auditory range.

The higher the frequency and the shorter the wavelength, the greater the kinetic or physical power of the wave. At high frequencies electromagnetic waves can cut through steel. Longer waves have little physical power but carry huge amounts of universal intelligence. To communicate best with this intelligence, we use the longer waves.

In accordance with the law of universal harmony, the energy you radiate will determine the level of universal intelligence you can contact, and therefore bring back to your subconscious mind. Your brain waves are a precise indicator of the quality of energy you are radiating. The longer the wave and the higher the amplitude, the more powerful the universal intelligence you contact.

The only known instrument on earth that can tune into these longest waves and bring to you the incredible universal intelligence they contain is your paraconscious mind! When your mind is producing predominantly theta and delta brain waves, it is maximally tuning into universal power and intelligence. When your brain is predominantly in delta and operating at 1 cps, you are sending out brain waves 186,282 miles long. These longest waves vibrate with the greatest portion of the universal mind. Each brain wave you send out returns with intelligence from the universal mind for your use. When you add the voltage of high excitement to the longest brain waves, you have the best of all conditions for tuning into universal intelligence.

However, the universal intelligence in your subconscious mind must be directly experienced before it can become a part of you and be of any value. The only way you can experience it is to act on it by putting it to use in your daily life. Only when you take action and creatively experience the universal intelligence in your own life does it become a permanent part of your self.

From the Universal to the Personal

The various steps of applied active meditation are powerful because they give you access to the universal mind without the filter of conscious thought. You don't have to experience something first in the physical world for it to be real to your paraconscious mind. This opens the whole world of universal intelligence and power to you.

Up until now you have been conditioned to let your conscious mind predominate in the way you function. Almost everything in your subconscious mind was put there by your conscious mind alone and, thus, came only from the material world available to your five physical senses. As long as the input to your subconscious mind is determined by your conscious mind, the input from your paraconscious mind to your subconscious mind will be completely blocked, or too weak to be of use.

For paraconscious input to the subconscious mind to be strong enough to be usable, the overwhelming input from the conscious mind must be stopped or greatly reduced. Then, and only then, can the paraconscious input gain access to the subconscious storehouse with sufficient power for awareness and usage.

But the conscious mind does have an important role to play in increasing your personal power. If the paraconscious mind rules to the exclusion of the conscious mind, no action can be taken on the paraconscious input. The conscious mind is required for universal intelligence to be put into action. Paraconscious input will stay locked away in the subconscious archives until the conscious mind uses it to act creatively. Once the action is taken, another circuit of self-empowerment is completed.

Psycho-physical Rehearsal,
an Experience of the Mind

In this chapter you will learn to use psycho-physical rehearsal, parts one and two. All psycho-physical rehearsals have the same purpose, which is to bring intelligence from the universal mind to you. It is up to you to use that universal intelligence in your daily life.

Research has shown that mentally experiencing an activity can affect the body the same way as actual performance of it. Early research was conducted on muscles alone and used biofeedback instruments. People sat in comfortable chairs and visualized a series of physical exercises. Their muscles did not move. Nevertheless, the biofeedback instruments registered the same during the visualization as they did during actual physical exercise.

More research has shown that all areas of performance benefit from visualization. By experiencing something mentally, you can effect the results you will achieve when you actually take action. You can mentally rehearse anything: the way your body moves, the way your emotions run, the way your thoughts proceed.

The idea of psycho-physical rehearsal is to experience something prior to its actual happening. Any kind of experience—physical, emotional or mental—is appropriate for psycho-physical rehearsal.

Psycho-physical rehearsal applies to anything you would like to become an expert at—to have full capacity at. You will be using your total mind, and will actually experience, probably for the first time in your life, achievement of whatever you desire. Psycho-physical rehearsal is your method for discovering potential and developing the ability to achieve a total and full life.

Psycho-physical rehearsal has been used extensively and successfully in sports. The popular term for this is the "inner game" of tennis, golf, football, etc. All these inner games do the sport first in a mental state in order to improve physical actions before using them. You can use psycho-physical rehearsal to dramatically improve your potential for any situation in which you expect to find yourself!

It can be done almost anywhere and at any time. You don't need to withdraw from humankind. You can perform your normal activities at the same time you are applying the technique. Once learned, psycho-physical rehearsal allows you to gain direct access to intelligence from the universal mind and transform it into your own personal power—at will. Whenever you use this technique to transcend a problem or obtain a desire, you not only meet your immediate goal, you also increase your inner resources for future use.

Access to a Great Source of Information

The late great Napoleon Hill, whose writings and research on success have helped so many, stated that the major difference between a genius and the average person is not that the genius is more brilliant or more educated. The difference, according to Dr. Hill, is the genius has access to a source of information and intelligence that the average person does not. Dr. Hill called this source of information infinite intelligence. We call it universal mind.

The universal mind has direction. It is creative. Each time you complete a psycho-physical rehearsal cycle, you add creative intelligence to your present intelligence. This increases your level of consciousness, your inner resources and your power. Thus with the completion of each psycho-physical rehearsal cycle, you create a new you with greater power and intelligence than existed before.

For example, suppose you desire more financial success. Psycho-physical rehearsal will help you to design and put into action a plan for achieving this. Suppose you wish to run your business more effectively. Psycho-physical rehearsal will put you in contact with the universal mind, which will, after it is transformed into your own personal intelligence, help you to design your plan of action for achieving a higher level of effectiveness. Suppose you are a sales rep. There is no greater sales tool than applying psycho-physical rehearsal to each specific sales situation before and during its actual occurrence.

In the complex area of human relationships, psycho-physical rehearsal can build bridges rather than walls, can move you toward cooperation and away from conflict. It can even help build love.

With the first psycho-physical rehearsal, you will learn to add intelligence from the universal mind to whatever is occurring in your life right now. With the second psycho-physical rehearsal, you will learn to add intelligence from the universal mind to the future events in your life.

Psycho-physical Rehearsal, Part One— More Power Now

With this psycho-physical rehearsal, you add intelligence from the universal mind to whatever you are doing at the time you are doing it. You draw on the universal mind to give direction to the situation in which you find yourself.

Sometimes when I am talking to a patient, for example, I feel as if a dose of intelligence from the universal mind would help in my interaction. The technique I use is this: Over the patient's right shoulder I project a horizon like the one I use in the cosmic review. On the horizon, I place my second self and the patient. Then I see and hear that second self talking to my patient. I see and hear this at the same time I am talking to the patient before me.

While talking to the patient, I passively observe the way my second self is acting with my patient. My conscious mind adds nothing to what is occurring between my second self and my patient. What I see happening on my horizon is what the universal mind would have me do at this time in this situation. After seeing and experiencing what occurs on my horizon, I then actually apply that knowledge to my actions with the patient in front of me. This way I get immediate feedback about the effectiveness of my psycho-physical rehearsal.

The entire process is very similar to the cosmic review. The main difference is you take immediate action, and therefore get immediate feedback on how powerful the psycho-physical rehearsal was. There can be no better or faster feedback. The basic steps are:

1. Set up your horizon and project the current situation onto it.

2. Stop conscious input by becoming an observer. Send your second self into the scene. Keep yourself outside the scene as an observer, not adding any conscious input.

3. Observe the occurrences on the horizon. This is input from your paraconscious mind.

4. Take the actions you have observed and apply them immediately to the situation you're in.

5. You now have completed a circuit of self-empowerment.

6. You now get an immediate response to your psycho-physical rehearsal. Being immediate it is the most wonderful feedback you can get on how effective your rehearsal was.

Psycho-physical Rehearsal, Part Two—More Power for the Future

The process for applying psycho-physical rehearsal to upcoming events has similar steps. Let's take the example of an important meeting that is scheduled for tomorrow. Use your conscious mind to project the meeting room onto your horizon. Insert your second self into that room. Initially direct your second self to experience the room itself. Does anything feel uncomfortable? Let your second self work to alleviate the discomfort.

Experience the people in the room individually, then as a group. Next experience the material you wish to present and discuss, and finally what actions will take place, and how universal intelligence can lead you to the results you most desire.

Remember that the input from your conscious mind is at an end once the scene is put on your horizon. You then watch what happens. You are an observer. You do not enter the scene. Watch your second self, which is acting according to intelligence from the universal mind. When the scene has played out, use your journal to record your observations.

On the day of the meeting, you will feel at ease. You have been here before and you know what to do. You will be taking into that meeting the actions and insights suggested by the universal mind. Due to your use of psycho-physical rehearsal, you will have the highest intelligence and power in the universe as your partner for the meeting.

You always have the option of doing another psycho-physical rehearsal during the meeting. Thus as the meeting progresses, you can continue to add intelligence from the universal mind. As different situations arise, universal power will be there to help you by adding its ideas, suggestions and insights to your subconscious mind.

Do you have worries, doubts and fears about the upcoming meeting? What better way to transcend them than in a psycho-physical rehearsal *before* the actual meeting. Rather than reacting to these worries, fears and doubts you have replaced them with high excitement, high expectation and high anticipation. When you combine universal intelligence with excitement and confidence, there is no better script for success.

Steps in Psycho-physical Rehearsal— Part Two

As you can see, the psycho-physical rehearsal is a way to make creative intelligence from the universal mind a constant part of your daily life. You do not limit meditation to an hour in a chair at the end of the day. With psycho-physical rehearsal, you use meditation, your paraconscious mind and universal creative intelligence all day, everyday. Psycho-physical rehearsal gives you the ability to add universal power to your life any time you need or desire it. It is one of the greatest sources of power known. It is a one-way street to abundance.

The psycho-physical rehearsal, part two, consists of four steps:

1. Set up your horizon and project the future situation onto it.

2. Stop conscious input by becoming an observer. Send your second self into the scene. Keep your first self outside the scene as an observer, not adding any conscious input.

3. Observe the occurrences on the horizon. The interactions you are seeing and hearing are from the universal mind, through your paraconscious. Keep experiencing them until any feelings of discomfort are eased and until you have experienced a successful encounter. You should feel empowered, competent and excited at the conclusion of the psycho-physical rehearsal.

4. Act on the new intelligence you have received from the universal. Your conscious mind will direct the action that is dictated once you feel comfortable and competent with the

things and people in the environment on your horizon. Act spontaneously, without fear or doubt, without letting outdated belief systems hold you back. Once you take this action in your everyday life, you have completed the circuit of self-empowerment.

Whenever you complete a psycho-physical rehearsal, your body radiates energy back into the surrounding universe. This energy then vibrates with and brings back to you the universal energy with which it is in harmony. The more powerful your radiation, the more powerful the universal intelligence it will bring you.

Review and Summary of the Psycho-physical Rehearsal of Future Events

In general, the psycho-physical rehearsal of the future consists of five separate but totally related psycho-physical rehearsals. In the first your second self responds to the environment. It makes any changes necessary so the environment becomes comfortable to your second self. After creating a comfortable environment your second self goes into the second psycho-physical rehearsal.

Your second self now looks at and interacts individually with each of the people you believe will be there. Respond to each of them as you believe them to be, never as you wish them to be. You can also add people, real or fictional, who will be annoying to you or supporting of you. By so doing you can see how universal intelligence would respond to your projected annoyances and supports. You will now be prepared to respond to whatever occurs with the power and wisdom of universal intelligence at your side.

Now follow with a psycho-physical rehearsal of the individual people, of your second self interacting with the entire group. At the completion of that, the next psycho-physical rehearsal is on whatever you expect to present at this meeting. What objections and approvals would you anticipate, and how would universal intelligence react to them? Become an observer. Let universal intelligence show you some possible objections or approvals you would never think of. In addition, experience what presentations or actions you might expect from others, and rehearse your response along with that of universal intelligence.

Finally, have your second self respond to the actions that take place at the meeting or whatever environment the psycho-physical rehearsal is in. You now have covered the environment, the individual people, the group collectively, the presentations—plus the responses to them and possible plans of action. You have completed the psycho-physical rehearsal.

If at the end your mind has anything in it other than positive thoughts and success—if you feel anything other than high excitement, anticipation and expectations—you still have not replaced all of your conscious mind's doubts, fears and worries. Redo the psycho-physical rehearsal until you identify them, devalue them, and replace them. You will know when this is so because your mind will be filled only with visions of success; your feelings will be only of high excitement, anticipation and expectation.

More Power and Radiance

Every living thing radiates energy from itself. Your personal radiation follows the law of universal harmony. It vibrates with those waves of universal intelligence you are in harmony with.

Your personal radiation is like a boomerang. Being born of you, it returns to you. When it returns it brings with it the power of harmonious universal intelligence. The more powerful your radiation, the more powerful the radiation of the universal mind it will vibrate with and bring back to you!

Each complete psycho-physical rehearsal cycle increases both the personal power you have available and the power of your next radiation. Each day you therefore become more powerful and more radiant. You are evolving. Your journal will reflect your progress.

You will never arrive at a final destination. You may achieve specific results, but you will always be moving on to a higher level of living, whichever one is next for you. Each day of your life, psycho-physical rehearsal offers you the opportunity to become more joined with the universal energy that created you. How wonderful to be aware of this, and by this awareness, to have the opportunity of experiencing it every day of your life!

The Fallacy of Aging

Do you believe you can grow old without aging? There is no question that our bodies age. Most of us think we must lose most—if not all—of our capabilities with the passing years. But I know that everyone can add many productive years to life, years that can be virtually free of disease and pain. If we are aware only of our physical bodies, we can't help but age as we grow older. But when we become aware of our total selves, we can grow older and increase our capabilities with each passing day. The difference depends entirely on the process by which you live.

When you use the meditations in this book, you are continuously in contact with the universal mind—constantly manifesting its power creatively in your daily life. You are continuously evolving to higher levels of consciousness. Living this process is, in my opinion, the purpose of life.

The success of our life is not determined by how many years our physical body remains alive and functioning. The success of our life is constantly gathering more and more intelligence from the universal mind and transforming it into our own personal power. When you live in order to receive intelligence, you will discover that each age gives you a unique situation and environment for your purposes. The intelligence from the universal mind you are capable of processing at age twenty is very different from that at age sixty. Believe me, I've lived through both of them!

At each age, you have the opportunity to expand your awareness and consciousness and become more universally intelligent as a total person. As a consequence, you will be more powerful, even though your kinetic or physical power is decreasing. If you lose physical power each year and gain nothing or very little in universal intelligence and power, you age. You stagnate. You deteriorate. Your body is part of the material world and must, according to the second law of thermodynamics, progress from order to disorder—ending in the final disorder we call death. Aging is a tragedy only when you do not match the increasing disorder of your body with an increasing evolution of your total self. When you do match becoming older with an increasing self-evolution, aging becomes a glorious opportunity to add to your powers!

Psycho-physical rehearsal is a basic life process. It is a way to achieve success and joy on earth while assuring the evolution of your eternal self. Once you learn psycho-physical rehearsal, you can transcend aging. You can replace it with continually greater self-evolution, self-development, and self-fulfillment.

Thought Patterns and Psycho-physical Rehearsal

Psycho-physical rehearsal gives you the power to achieve and do what you previously could not. If you have trouble accomplishing something, your problem probably lies in your attitude toward that thing. You may have been told you were incapable of doing it. You may have tried it once and been less than successful. Your conscious mind now tells you that you are incapable of doing it—that you are not good enough. You begin to question your capabilities. The more you question, the more you doubt, and the more willing you become to listen to the negative input of others.

Most of the time, if there is a specific thing you would like to do or to achieve, you do not spontaneously go after it. Instead, you listen to your conscious mind, which tells you to pause and take a look at how the experts would go about it. Then you begin comparing yourself with these experts. If you have never done the thing before, naturally you will come up short. With any comparison you put yourself in a state of competition. You begin to doubt that you are good enough. If there is anything that can drain your energy, it is this comparison and competition.

You will be much better off when you turn to your paraconscious mind *before* you even consider looking anywhere else for information on how to proceed. When you receive the input of your paraconscious mind, you become aware of your own inherent qualities and powers. You may perceive some doubts, but you will discover what that doubting is all about. You will usually find that the roots of any doubts you have are based on the opinions of others about your capabilities.

Remember, ours is a bipolar universe, a universe of matching negatives and positives. And when they are joined we create a current and energy flows. For every fear, doubt and worry we have, universal intelligence has powerful visions, excitement and expectations. And remember also—each and every time we *replace* anything inappropriate, our success and powers grow. We become more.

When you use psycho-physical rehearsal to encourage input from your paraconscious mind, three things occur. First, you become aware of your present doubts and comparisons and their sources. Second, you become aware of the inherent powers you have. Third, you gain new powers from the new paraconscious input.

Process: the Most Important Part

To do a psycho-physical rehearsal of anything, you must pay attention to the process rather than the outcome. The result you hope to attain is of secondary importance. To begin the process, the first step is to create an environment. Do not assume what that environment should be. If for instance, your goal is to call on the universal mind to help you make a painting, you will project your horizon and then find an appropriate environment for painting. A studio may appear. If the furnishings in that studio keep changing shape, go with the changes. Let them happen. It is not unusual for the images in a psycho-physical rehearsal to change. The first image you put up there on your horizon was probably influenced by your conscious mind using the material available from your subconscious mind. Future changes that occur will be from the universal mind operating through your paraconscious mind.

The studio you've placed on your horizon may change into an outdoor scene, a beautiful forest with squirrels darting around. The universal mind is showing you the environment in which you can do your best painting. Your initial idea that you would be in a studio to paint was probably based on what authorities told you. You had that notion filed away in your subconscious mind. Your conscious mind went to the file, found the idea about the studio and put it up on the horizon as the proper setting for your psycho-physical rehearsal of painting. Your paraconscious mind, free of the stagnation of belief systems, knows a better environment for you and sends that picture to your subconscious mind.

When you become more experienced at psycho-physical rehearsal, you will often not use your conscious mind to set up the environment. Your paraconscious mind and the universal mind will set it up for you from the start.

The Experience of Spontaneity

One of the most important benefits of the psycho-physical rehearsal is learning to take immediate and spontaneous action on the intelligence from the universal mind that your paraconscious mind brings you. Doing psycho-physical rehearsals trains you to stop the conscious mind's interfering input and allow the paraconscious mind to function.

In the above example of psycho-physical rehearsal, the paraconscious immediately changed the studio environment to a forest. Your job as an observer is to let the change unfold. You spontaneously accept what the paraconscious mind shows you.

The other option is to allow your conscious mind to question whether you should paint in the forest. Your conscious mind can raise such doubts as: *It would be difficult to take your easel and paints outdoors, so think twice before considering such a stupid move. Logically you have decided on the studio for this painting, so don't be dissuaded from logic by some silly intuition or daydream. Never pay attention to these fantasy daydreams. They have no relation to reality.*

With these doubts from the conscious mind, communication with the universal mind through the paraconscious immediately ceases. If, instead, you respond immediately to the change in location, you are acting spontaneously. Spontaneity is a vital part of psycho-physical rehearsal. It is also vital for any method you use to increase your personal power. Psycho-physical rehearsal is your training ground for spontaneity. It gives you the opportunity to understand, to experience and finally to respond spontaneously in safety.

The Experience of Non-attachment

Non-attachment is another essential concept in the whole process of applied active meditation. With psycho-physical rehearsal, you can actually experience non-attachment, and thereby know what it feels like and what it is. When you practice achieving non-attachment in the world of the psycho-physical rehearsal, you will be an expert at it when you need it in the world of material reality.

Non-attached does not mean detached. Detached means you do not care, and take no action. If you are non-attached, you care a great deal and you do take action, but your emotions are free to be used in any direction you like. When you are attached, your emotions are directed one way and are not free to change directions. When you become non-attached, your emotions are free to move in whatever direction you feel is most appropriate and productive.

For example, suppose someone does something injurious to you or your family. You hate that person with a vengeance. Your hate is directed at and completely attached to that person. Your hate requires a great deal of energy to keep it focused on that one individual. Since that energy is attached to the person you hate, you are limited in how you can use it. You can use it to try to injure the person you hate. Or if you cannot injure that individual, you can just let it swell up inside of you, leaving little room for anything else. Retained emotions are an enormous drain of energy. The energy drain of strong repressed emotions makes appropriate actions almost impossible.

When strong emotions are retained, they also affect the functioning of the physical body. Most emotions, and especially fears, first affect the adrenal glands and then the urinary tract, kidneys and colon. Hate, envy and jealousy directly affect the spleen, which is your reserve battery, the reserve power source of your body. Your spleen also draws out iron and produces red blood cells. It is important for the functioning of your immune system. When your immune system is impaired, you are open to disease. So retaining hate, or any strong negative emotion, weakens you in almost all functions and increases your susceptibility to disease.

Emotion is energy in motion. When you repress an emotion it de-energizes you. You also become attached to repressed emotions and they hold you fast. When you decide not to express an emotion, you rob it of its ability to move and to energize you. You attach it to something that holds it fast. Becoming non-attached is basic for increasing personal power. Your psycho-physical rehearsal is one of the best and most effective training grounds for learning the process of freeing your emotions from debilitating attachments.

Instead of directing your new increase in energy toward hitting the nose of the person you hate, use it to increase your competence at transcending. You use it to increase your ability to respond to any situation. As a result of freeing your energy and using it for self-development, you are a person more in control of yourself than one controlled by negative emotions.

Reaction Versus Response

For almost every occurrence in your life you have two options: you can react or you can respond. Which you choose will determine your success, your achievements and, most important, the quality of your life. The difference between reacting and responding is the difference between using part of your mind and using your total mind. It is also the difference between being attached and being non-attached.

When you react, you direct your emotion toward the situation that provoked the reaction. Whether you react to hate by punching the offending person or using that energy to clean your desk, you are still reacting. Therefore, you are tied to the situation that caused you to hate. Your emotions are not free to flow away from their cause.

When you react, you are operating on assumptions. Reaction occurs when you use only the conscious and subconscious aspects of your mind. With your conscious mind you are aware of, and in contact with, only what is happening in your material life at the present moment. Your conscious mind draws on the archives in your subconscious to interpret occurrences in your life. It is limited to your previous experiences and what you've been taught. To see beyond what you already know, you must use your paraconscious mind.

When you rely exclusively on your conscious-subconscious mind, as events occur, immediately there comes this little image of how you were treated before. You assume you will be treated the same way this time. Then you react to what you assume is happening or about to happen by going into a state of defense. Reaction is always defensive.

When you react to any situation, even so-called good events, you become attached. When you assume a threat and react to it, your entire body chemistry focuses on one set of assumptions. These assumptions have become so enormous, they have so filled your mind, that nothing else can enter. You are attached to them. You cannot go beyond them. You are stagnated, and your radiant energy drops to very low levels.

When you live a life of reacting, you are constantly walking around in a state of readiness. *Somebody out there is going to take advantage of me—is going to do harm to me—is going to compete with me and defeat me.* So you are always fighting, always competing, always in readiness to make the other guy a loser and yourself a winner. The disharmony and damage resulting from such a view injures you and the entire world.

When you walk around in a state of readiness, your muscles contract. Your nervous system contracts. Your brain and mind contract. The power of your radiation drops sharply. With such contraction, with such weak energy radiation, you can only know and be aware of what is happening in your immediate local environment. When you are so contracted that your voltage goes down, so does your resistance to outside forces. You become vulnerable to everything from bacteria to disease, from constant fear to a host of mental and emotional problems.

When you *respond* to a situation, you don't immediately strike out in one direction. Before taking action or making decisions, you stop your conscious mind's input and seek feedback from your paraconscious mind. This way you add universal intelligence and its power to the situation before taking any action. With the addition of such power to your decision-making and actions, you are far more effective and robust than if you're a slave to reaction.

The power and insight you gain from your paraconscious input remains a part of you, for your use whenever needed. By using psycho-physical rehearsal to respond rather than your emotions react, you transcend the emotion and its original cause, and move to a higher, more effective plane of living.

When strong emotions arise, they create an abundance of energy. When the energy created is non-attached and free to move, it can be used to transcend the cause of the emotion, and thus increase personal power. This is true of happy and good emotions as well as irritating ones. If you become attached to a joy and want to keep repeating that feeling for the rest of your life, you will be blocking the flow of your energy as much as if you were attached to a negative emotion. You will be limiting yourself to your present happiness, and preventing an inflow of even greater joys.

When you react you are living in a unipolar world. You see only the problem. When you respond you are living in a bipolar world. You see both the problem and its opposite appropriate vision in universal intelligence. You experience the whole picture, taking action to replace the inappropriate problem with an appropriate vision.

Every psycho-physical rehearsal is a response, not a reaction. You are responding to an event that either has happened, is occurring presently or will occur. By contacting the universal mind and bringing forth its intelligence, you see the bipolar picture and set your energy free to flow in the direction that will bring you the most wisdom and power. Psycho-physical rehearsal develops your ability to experience the bipolar world, to respond to the whole world. It allows you to achieve both non-attachment and spontaneity and, thus, a lifetime of continual personal evolution.

Repetition, Repetition, Repetition

The place to start practicing non-attachment is within the scene you create for your psycho-physical rehearsal. As you observe the setting of the event you're rehearsing—be it an event occurring in the present or one that will occur—register your responses to everything in that setting. Be aware of your five senses of seeing, hearing, smelling, tasting and feeling. Notice which ones are stimulated. Get all you can out of your initial observations of the setting. Note your level of comfort or discomfort: those specific aspects that contribute to your comfort and those that contribute to your discomfort. Note if the comfort or discomfort affects your body. What do you feel? Do you experience areas of excitement or areas of blockage? Where are they? When you become proficient with your psycho-physical rehearsals, you can actually discover how your body is physiologically functioning. At this beginning level, however, just tune in to what extent you are aware of your body functions.

Perceive yourself as really being in the environment you have created. You must experience the psycho-physical rehearsal as reality. As soon as you feel you have examined all aspects of the environment and your relationship to it, then consciously withdraw.

Note what happens to you during this state of withdrawal. Remove yourself from the environment. Then, mentally erase whatever is left of the environment. Become aware of any thoughts now coming to you. Prepare again to focus on the environment and to go back into it.

Why go back into the same environment? Your first trip into an environment is like a scouting expedition. You have to find your way in unfamiliar territory. You have to learn how to adapt. Most people, when they first perceive and experience an unfamiliar environment, feel nervous. This is normal. It's also why you let yourself out of the environment, then go back for another look. The first time you can miss a lot of things that might hamper you later on. The second time there should be less nervousness because a certain adaptation and familiarization have already occurred.

When the environment occurs again, notice what comes back. See if any changes are already taking place. Are you feeling more familiar with it? Now again put yourself into it. Explore by moving around. Focus on the details. See if you can find any new details since your last visit. You may discover some more things that make you uncomfortable. The situation was so new the first time, and you were so nervous you did not realize some other discomfort.

When you feel disturbed by what you encounter, continue to familiarize yourself with it until you see how to handle it. Then get away from it and go back again, and see how well you handle it this time. Is it still disturbing, or can you now handle it and move on? This is a further step in your non-attachment training. When you cannot handle it, you are attached to it. When you become non-attached, you allow in the power to handle it.

This non-attachment can occur quite rapidly. You can adapt quickly once you feel the environment is not as threatening as it seemed in the first encounter.

Facing a Hostile Environment

Right away you probably hoped to find a nice environment that was suitable for your pursuits. Please don't expect this from the psycho-physical rehearsal. If you're like most people, you have made enormous efforts in your life to change everything and everybody in your environment so it is safe and suitable for you. You have the crazy idea the world should be set up according to your desires. If the environment is hostile, you're not going to blame yourself for not being able to handle it. You are going to blame it and the people connected with it. They are causing your problems, not you. And you are going to try to change them. You are also going to try to change whatever else in your environment is at the root of your disease.

But the point of psycho-physical rehearsal is to make changes in yourself so you become capable of living well in any environment. It is fine to say, hey, this is not the best environment and I want to see it improved. The greatest improvement will come, however, when you change *yourself* so you can handle that environment. First, go to work on familiarizing yourself with that environment as it is so you will not be fixated on what is causing you trouble. Then allow your paraconscious mind to bring universal intelligence to bear on the environment.

A marvelous and supportive environment will not teach you how to handle your fears and anxieties. Psycho-physical rehearsal allows you to encounter your fears and anxieties so they lose their power over you. You free all the emotion trapped in attachment to particulars, and you become stronger.

I know the paralyzing effect fear can have. I have a lot of fears. But I'm grateful for them because I can use them in psycho-physical rehearsal to grow and evolve. Every time I experience a fear, it is a challenge for me to do something about it. And almost invariably, once I have faced my fear, I realize it was not totally valid to begin with. With psycho-physical rehearsal, rather than push fear away and try to avoid it, I respond to and transcend it and, thus, use it to build my personal power. Rather than reacting, I respond to the fear by tuning into the universal mind. Then I let my paraconscious bring intelligence from the universal mind into my subconscious. I complete the circuit by taking the action directed by my conscious mind, staying with the fear until all its negative effects have been overcome by my increased personal power.

Through the psycho-physical rehearsal we learn to see the bipolar universe we live in. When we see an inappropriate action in our daily life, at the same time we see a clear vision of an appropriate action in the universal mind. When we join the two together in our mind, we produce a tremendous creative power. This creative power, with great intensity, now seeks expression in the world of our daily life. Use this power. When you use it you transform it into your own personal power, and then you have the power to successfully handle almost any environment you ever encounter.

The Importance of Intent

The nature of your intent for every psycho-physical rehearsal is paramount. By intent, I mean your reason for doing the exercise. Are you doing it to increase your own competence? To raise your own level of consciousness? Or are you doing it to beat someone else? For instance, perhaps I want to do something better because I'm embarrassed when you outperform me in public. I am jealous of you. I have some envy. I may even be spiteful. Rather than being in competition with myself, being interested in improving myself, my intent is to be in competition with you so I will look better than you. And I might succeed and actually outdo you. But I still have my envy, spite and jealousy. Therefore I will have improved in a particular situation, but I will not have transcended the negative emotions that led me to seek that improvement in the first place. I will always encounter people who can do certain things better than I can. Again I will feel envy, spite and jealousy.

If, however, my intent is to transcend my envy, spite and jealousy, then when I add intelligence from the universal mind to myself, I become more powerful. I will have proper actions to take. I will have removed the envy, spite and jealousy not by trying to lessen their power, but by increasing my power until I am completely non-attached to them. As long as my energy is attached to the envy, spite and jealousy, it is not free for me to use. Once I obtain sufficient intelligence and power to free the energy bound by these emotions, then I can apply that energy to any area of my life that I choose.

When my intent is to experience the bipolar reality of each inappropriate occurrence in my life, I will see the appropriate vision with which to replace it. When I replace my inappropriate experience with the appropriate vision from my bipolar experience, I have created a wiser and more powerful me.

Another very important reason for evaluating your intent is to make sure whether at this time you should be doing what you are doing in your psycho-physical rehearsal. If you keep rehearsing and rehearsing, and what you experience does not give you excitement and pleasure and joy, you are doing an inappropriate psycho-physical rehearsal. If you say you want to do a painting, but every time you rehearse it, you feel uncomfortable and feel no excitement, then you have to ask yourself if you really want to do that painting. The uncomfortable feeling and lack of excitement are telling you that you do not want to paint. The uncomfortable feeling tells you that you still may be attached. The lack of excitement tells you that for whatever reason your energy is not in motion and flowing. Under these conditions, whatever you do in the psycho-physical rehearsal or in real life will fail! When your psycho-physical rehearsal shows you that you are not yet ready to do something, put that goal aside for a time. Look for the fears, doubts and other negative emotions to which you are attached. Work on becoming non-attached. And work on building your personal power in all ways.

If you are getting ready to perform a specific event or feat and you aim your psycho-physical rehearsal at it, your intent must not be to have control over the one situation but rather to learn to have control over every situation. Therefore if your psycho-physical rehearsal is on a business meeting you are about to have, your desire should go beyond having a successful meeting to learning the process of psycho-physical rehearsal so you can empower yourself to face any situation.

You begin the actual psycho-physical rehearsal by establishing a specific goal. If your goal is to have a successful business meeting, then your paraconscious mind knows to get and bring to you the intelligence that you will need for your meeting. A specific goal gives you a target and the raw material you will use to begin your progress. You need not, however, limit what you achieve during your psycho-physical rehearsal to a specific goal. With input from the universal mind, you may achieve a result far beyond your original target. Or you may achieve more than one goal. The goal is just the bait by which you get the psycho-physical rehearsal going. The universal mind and the bipolar vision you respond to will determine how far you can go during one psycho-physical rehearsal.

The set of circumstances that you work with in your psycho-physical rehearsal should be as close to reality as possible. If one of the people attending your business meeting is very abusive and disruptive, to portray him as kind and cooperative would turn the psycho-physical rehearsal into a mockery. Your intent must be to represent the situation of the psycho-physical rehearsal to your paraconscious as accurately as possible.

Set up the environment of the meeting and become familiar with it. As you explore the environment, you will discover those factors that are interfering with your performance and those that are supporting you. Keep going back to the environment until you have overcome all the interference and are relaxed and in control. Now start into the actual meeting.

At your last business meeting, you were not successful. You felt incompetent to handle many of the problems that arose. For this meeting, first do a cosmic review of the last meeting. Let your paraconscious experience the situation in which you did so poorly. Let your paraconscious show you the bipolar picture. You will see an appropriate vision that achieves what your previous actions failed to achieve. Repeat that disastrous meeting as often as needed. With each repeat, you will become more relaxed and non-attached. You will finally experience yourself competently handling the meeting.

Immediately put your new power into use by rehearsing the upcoming meeting. Become familiar with how it really feels to have this meeting. With each rehearsal, you will make new discoveries and develop new powers. As you put these powers into action in your rehearsal, you'll feel more and more competent. You will learn how success feels.

Competence and Spontaneity

When, by doing the psycho-physical rehearsal, you come to know you are competent, your doubts and fears will dissolve—your faith, power and excitement will increase—and you will take action spontaneously. Once you act spontaneously and the results prove your competence, you will be even more willing to go immediately with the new input from your paraconscious. And so the upward spiral begins. Spontaneous action turns universal intelligence into personal intelligence. The ability to act spontaneously grows out of feelings of self-worth. Competence fuels those feelings. The more able you are, the more worthy you will feel, and the more spontaneously you will act. This spontaneity will increase your power, giving you even more competence and self-worth.

No matter what situation you rehearse, you are not training yourself just for that situation. You are training yourself to become competent in whatever comes along so you can have spontaneous articulation and action. With each psycho-physical rehearsal, you have a marvelous opportunity to experience and become aware of all those hidden things that prevent you from becoming competent.

The Mind's Habitat

You do not do your psycho-physical rehearsal in your head. It is very important that you project the actions outside yourself. Your created horizon will always be within your energy field. When you increase your radiance and power with psycho-physical rehearsals, you will experience your horizon moving farther away from you. This indicates that you are increasing your energy field, and hence your energy and power.

Where is your mind? Understanding the answer to this question is basic for psycho-physical rehearsal. Remember, you cannot *truly* understand the answers until you experience them. While I am now sharing knowledge with you, you will have true understanding only from your own experience. You will gain that experience by doing the cosmic review and psycho-physical rehearsals and putting your new powers into action.

The mind is within and without: It surrounds the body. It is the mediator, the link between the body and the universal mind. It communicates with both. However, the mind is also within. Its energy extends to every cell in the body. Therefore we have the oft-repeated statement from Jack Schwarz: *All of your body is in your mind, but not all of your mind is in your body.*

During psycho-physical rehearsal you are in touch with the mind, not just the brain. The brain is comparable to an amplifier. It magnifies the intelligence brought to it by the mind. It also transforms the energy from the mind into the biochemicals the body needs for life. When the power of universal intelligence activates the mind, the brain will produce the biochemicals of bodily health. When the universal intelligence inflow is blocked, the brain usually produces the biochemicals of disease.

You will find the psycho-physical rehearsal useful almost every day of your life. Now is the time to start.

Summary: The Psycho-physical Rehearsal, Part One—More Power Now

You wish to add universal intelligence and power to whatever you are currently doing. First, project a horizon. Onto that horizon, project your second self, what is now occurring in your life.

While you remain active in your current situation, you stop all conscious mind input from entering the scene occurring on your horizon. You observe what is happening on your horizon and what your second self is doing.

The actions occurring on your horizon are those that the universal mind is suggesting for you to take in your current situation. Spontaneously act on the suggestions from the universal mind. Do not hesitate. Allow no doubts, questions or fears. You will feel excitement, faith and high energy.

Since you are applying input from the universal mind immediately in your daily life, you will get immediate feedback on how effective your psycho-physical rehearsal is. Even though you achieve some success the first time you do this, remember you will achieve greater success each time you call on the psycho-physical rehearsal, even in this same situation. Each time you do, your power and success increases.

When you begin your meditations you will attain your weakest results. As you increase your personal power, the power of your results greatly increases. But we all must start at the beginning and take our first steps. Only then can we learn to sprint.

If ever you get nothing on your horizon or when the results from applying what you do get are unsuccessful, you know that you were not yet ready for the step you tried to take. You need more preparation. Go back to the cosmic review to discover what fears, belief systems and attachments are preventing you from progressing. Once you've used your cosmic reviews to remove your energy blocks and raise your power, you will get successful results with your psycho-physical rehearsal.

Summary: Psycho-physical Rehearsal, Part Two—More Power for the Future

Project onto your horizon the location in which the future event will occur. Project what you believe the place will look like and what objects you will encounter there. Project your second self into this place.

As you look around, ask yourself what in this place annoys you or seems inappropriate? Whenever you encounter an object that engenders these feelings, stay with it. The intelligence from the universal mind will bring you the vision and power needed to transcend the negative feelings. As is true with so much in life, you cannot change the thing, but you can increase your power to the point where the thing no longer offends or disturbs you. Where you take control rather than being controlled.

Once you feel comfortable with everything you have encountered, remove your second self from the projected location. Pause for a moment. Then send your second self back in. With each re-entry, you will discover things that you were not aware of on previous explorations. Repeat going in and out of the place until you have transcended any irritations.

Once you feel comfortable with everything you find in the projected location, you are ready to look at each of the people who will be there. Be sure to see them all as they really are, not as you would like them to be. Interact with anyone who causes you annoyance or discomfort. Call on the universal mind to guide your interaction.

Repeat your interaction with a person as long as there is any feeling of inappropriateness or any increase in the excitement level. When you no longer have inappropriate feelings and when your excitement level has stabilized, you have completed the necessary interactions with the people in the scene.

Now it's time to project the actual event that will occur, with all the objects and people in their places. Watch closely as the action unfolds. Stop all conscious input. Place your second self in the scene. Observe. Remember that once your conscious mind sets the scene, its job is done.

Repeat the event until you have the power to transcend any inappropriate actions that may be occurring. You now can experience yourself in control. You feel competent. You have transcended your worries and fears. You have the intelligence and power of your creator working within you.

You are prepared for the actual event when it occurs. You are excited. You feel and know your own powers. You couldn't be more ready.

A Reminder

Please remember that everything in this book is a generalized guide or map. You are unique and, therefore, you must adapt all these exercises to your particular needs. That's why the emphasis is on the process rather than the specifics of any situation. Situations will always change, but the process remains the same. As you develop your abilities you will be able to apply them to whatever you encounter. Success and abundance will become automatic.

6
AUTOGENIC PSYCHO-PHYSICAL REHEARSAL

> *To see a World in a Grain of Sand,*
> *And a Heaven in a Wild Flower,*
> *Hold Infinity in the palm of your hand,*
> *And eternity in an hour.*
> —William Blake, "Auguries of Innocence"

In the last chapter, you learned how to apply the two parts of the psycho-physical rehearsal to events—both immediate and in the future. When you add these techniques to the cosmic review, which you learned in Chapter 4, you have tools for applying intelligence from the universal mind to your past, present and future. The cosmic review and the two psycho-physical rehearsals you have learned are meant to be generated by specific events in your life. You use a past event, a current event or an event that you know is going to occur as the target for input from the universal mind. By putting the wisdom and power you receive into action in your everyday life, you complete a circuit of self-empowerment, thus increasing your personal wisdom and power.

The next level of applied active meditation is the autogenic psycho-physical rehearsal. Autogenic means self-generating. In the autogenic psycho-physical rehearsal, your mind itself generates the subject of the meditation. No specific event is necessary. Since the subject matter available to your mind has virtually no limit, you can apply the autogenic psycho-physical rehearsal to anything. This level of applied active meditation opens opportunities for you to complete exciting and powerful circuits of self-empowerment at any time, in any place, limited only by your desires and imagination.

You can use the meditation on an activity as commonplace as walking. You probably walk every day and view it as an ordinary experience, a simple means of getting from one place to another. With the autogenic psycho-physical rehearsal, you can turn walking into a circuit of self-empowerment. You can also sit in a chair and imagine you're walking and turn even that into a circuit of self-empowerment. There is almost nothing that cannot be used as bait for your paraconscious to cast into the universal mind.

You can use the autogenic psycho-physical rehearsal with symbols. Symbols themselves are not knowledge, but almost all symbols contain within them a great deal of knowledge. When you do a psycho-physical rehearsal on a symbol, you can receive enormous amounts of knowledge and wisdom.

With the autogenic psycho-physical rehearsal, you can have conversations with people who are not physically present. For example, Jack Schwarz is in Ashland, Oregon, and I am in Cleveland, Ohio. During the writing of this book, I wanted input from Jack many times. So I did an autogenic psycho-physical rehearsal. With my conscious mind I constructed a table and two chairs. I put Jack in one chair and myself in the other. Then I went into my paraconscious mind function, and Jack and I had long, productive discussions. Immediately after these sessions, I completed the circuit of self-empowerment by putting into writing what "he" and I had discussed.

I have also used the autogenic psycho-physical rehearsal to have conversations with people I have never met. After reading Ellen Langer's wonderful book, *Mindfulness*, I had a long and productive discussion with "her" at my usual table in the autogenic psycho-physical rehearsal. Other people with whom I've had productive sessions are Wayne Dyer, Viktor Frankl, Robert Ringer, Ralph Strauch, Ram Dass, and Bernard Jensen. The autogenic psycho-physical rehearsal has dramatically widened my circle of friends and allowed me to add circuits of self-empowerment to my life that no other procedure could produce.

I grew up reading William Blake, whose writings can be hard to interpret at times. I read many books on the meaning of Blake's work. I became a student of Blake and learned that Blake himself did what I would call autogenic psycho-physical rehearsals. He did not use that terminology, of course. But he did find ways of gaining access to other minds to help him in his work. He was once asked how he managed to become such a profound poet, having had no training in writing. He answered that he did not write poetry by himself. Whenever he wanted to write, he said, he called on the poet John Milton, who died nearly a hundred years before Blake was born, for advice.

For me, the final piece of the Blake puzzle was to sit down with the poet and discuss with him the meaning of his writings and their significance for my life. Yes, I actually asked William Blake to explain to me how I could apply certain lines of his poetry to my existence. And during the autogenic psycho-physical rehearsal, he gave me the explanations I needed. How do I know that I had a valid session with William Blake? When I put what I learned from him into action, my life was immediately enriched. For all meditations, results are the proof of their validity.

In *Think and Grow Rich,* Napoleon Hill describes a success technique he calls the power of the master mind. Dr. Hill's research showed that the most successful people were those who surrounded themselves with other people of great brain power. He found that when a group of such people was functioning in harmony, it created a large increase in energy, and that increased energy became available to every individual in the group. He called this "coordination of knowledge and effort, in a spirit of harmony, between two or more people for the attainment of a definite purpose, the master mind." When people combine their brain power to accomplish something, that master mind takes on a life of its own and is actually far more powerful than the sum of its parts.

With my own autogenic psycho-physical rehearsals I have formed many master mind groups with Dr. Hill, as well as with other people. By being in harmony with these people and interacting with them during the meditation, I have felt the creation of this new entity—the master mind. And when I took the actions recommended by the master mind, I got wonderful results. As soon as you begin experiencing your own master mind sessions, you will know what I'm talking about.

Moving Beyond the Conscious Mind

To do the autogenic psycho-physical rehearsal, you can either use your conscious mind to decide the subject or you can let your paraconscious mind pick one for you. To do the latter, you must first relax. Then stop all conscious mind input. Once you have stopped the conscious mind input to the subconscious you will receive feedback from the paraconscious. Relax and stop any inflow from the conscious mind. Then see what images or sounds appear. Whatever event, object or person you then become aware of is your paraconscious mind's suggestion for your autogenic psycho-physical rehearsal.

As with the cosmic review and parts one and two of the psycho-physical rehearsal, you must be an observer during the autogenic psycho-physical rehearsal. All conscious mind inflow is shut off. Witness the unfolding of the scene in front of you as you would a movie. Watch what is happening. Perceive it fully and as *real* experience. You will be observing and experiencing what the paraconscious has to tell you. With your conscious mind you are limited to re-experiencing and drawing assumptions from knowledge you have been given by others. With your conscious mind alone you can raise your level of consciousness very little. With the conscious mind you are attached to and bound by your past experiences and your present knowledge. Both of these combine to create doubts and fears, which prevent growth and evolution. By the input of the paraconscious mind you can go beyond what you have already experienced. With paraconscious input you are no longer attached to your past. You are free of the fears and doubts you have built into your past and into your conscious mind.

Your conscious mind brings news to you from only your material environment. This is the local news. To know the universal news, you must open your self to paraconscious mind inflow. The universal paraconscious input from the autogenic psycho-physical rehearsal is your gateway to greater awareness, leading to an enormous increase in your personal powers, and to much greater and more powerful internal resources.

The paraconscious function of your mind is never out of contact with the universal mind. Your mind never sleeps; it continuously radiates into the universal mind. By applied active meditation you open your subconscious mind to the continual conversation going on between your paraconscious mind function and the universal mind.

Expanding the Use of Your Mind

The major achievement of the psycho-physical rehearsal is that you alter how you use your mind. You expand its use from two-thirds to your whole, total mind. With the input of the paraconscious mind, you begin to establish self-knowledge and to recognize that by which you have been needlessly limiting yourself. By adding universal power to your personal power, you transcend your old limits and raise your personal powers to a new level.

With your total mind, you can transcend all your old tapes and expand them into patterns of much greater power. You are no longer limited to the present connections and neurotransmitters in your nervous system. With the paraconscious function you can build new ones! You don't have to keep going over and over the same old limited power patterns. If you are dissatisfied for whatever reason, you don't have to sit and cry about it, or ask for "expert" help. You can do something about it now!

Don't throw out your old blueprints and patterns. Expand them. You transcend your old blueprints into ones of greater power, of greater harmony and personal evolution. This is where you start to restructure yourself into a transcendent self, continually living on higher levels of consciousness.

Rather than reacting to life with only your conscious-subconscious mind, you respond with your total mind. Thus, almost every action in your life is an opportunity for you to respond. And every response using your total mind is an opportunity for transcendence to a higher, more fulfilling, more blissful level of living.

The following exercises and meditations are designed to guide you to develop your ability to create autogenic psycho-physical rehearsals. If you are working alone, I suggest you read them into a tape-recorder and then play the tape and follow along. If you are working with a partner, have your partner take you through each exercise.

Exercises in Using the
Autogenic Psycho-physical Rehearsal

The first three exercises are prototypes for almost any autogenic psycho-physical rehearsal. The purpose of using walking as the first exercises is to take something that has no apparent excitement to it, something that offers nothing in the way of a challenge or little apparent chance for greater awareness and self-expansion—and show how such a mundane activity can be used for transformation.

Once you have learned how to expand your awareness through walking, you can apply the process to other everyday activities, such as washing the dishes, mopping the floors or attending boring meetings. When you can turn ordinary activities into circuits of self-empowerment, you have created for yourself a life of self-expansion and achievement that is never ending.

The first exercise requires that you actually move your body in accordance with the instructions. While you are moving, please be acutely aware of your body and what is happening within it. Many people have used this exercise to increase their awareness of their physical being to the point where they know exactly how each organ is functioning. I tell you this so you know just what is possible. But I don't intend for you to reach such a level of internal body awareness at this time. Just be as in-tune with your physical being as possible.

Also be aware of your feelings during this exercise. Do you feel in control of your life? Are you doing the exercise because you feel you should be? Or because you have been ordered to? Do you feel you are being controlled rather than being in control?

When you feel either controlled or obligated—for any reason—to do anything, you are operating predominantly in your conscious mind. To the extent that these feelings persist, there will be little if any paraconscious input. People who feel controlled or obligated do not evolve. This exercise, or any psycho-physical rehearsal, presents an opportunity for you to become aware of any conscious mind input that may be holding you back and to replace it with paraconscious mind inflow that gives you the freedom to expand and become more.

You can use this exercise, for instance, if you drive to work and then walk from your car to your office. As you walk, notice what is happening in your body and how you feel. Make an effort to take control of your feelings and to develop them in the directions you prefer. If you want to evolve to higher levels, you must first become aware of what is going on with you where your are and then know how to take control of your life. These exercises will begin to move you in that direction.

With the meditations we have done so far, you can take almost any situation at almost any time and use it to create a bipolar circuit of creative power. When you feel controlled, stop the conscious mind inflow creating this feeling. Complete a bipolar circuit by opening your mind to the inflow from the paraconscious mind. You will be shown a universal vision of what you need to do or think, or whatever, for you to take control. As soon as you put that vision into action you complete your circuit of self-empowerment and you are in control! Wow. Is anything more important in life than developing the ability to transcend being controlled by other people, events, fears, desires, etc. And this approach can be used to transcend any negative feelings you experience.

Now for the first exercise. Remember, you are actually moving your body in accordance with the instructions. You will be walking, marching and running in place.

Walking Exercise Number 1

Stand up.

March in place. Feel your legs going up and down. Note everything that you feel.

Now step up your pace. March a bit faster. Stay tuned in to the way the movement feels.

Now march as fast as you can. Pick up your feet as rapidly as possible. Pump your arms. Notice what full speed feels like.

Slow down to your original pace. Imagine you have spotted your destination. You can finally see it. Feel a sense of impatience to get there. You're almost there. Right up ahead, that's where you're going. You are now moving very fast and excitedly. *Very fast.*

You have arrived. Slow down and enjoy this spot that you've been so eager to reach. Savor the moment.

But wait. They're calling you to return to the place you came from. You've got to go back. You'd better pick up the pace. Their calls seem urgent. You're excited to let them know what you've found on your trip. You have great stories to tell them. Go as fast as you can.

Okay, you're back. You can stop.

Write about this exercise in your journal. What did you feel while performing the exercise? Describe all that you can.

When others have done this marching in place at different speeds, they have reported a range of feelings. Here's a sampling:

I felt my heart speed up.
I felt more free. I felt the muscles in my arms and legs.
I felt an increase in my circulation. A lot of physical energy. Felt myself wake up.
I felt I wanted to keep going. First I felt how heavy my legs were. Then I saw myself walking.
I did not know what I was supposed to feel.

This last reply has great meaning for us all. That person said she was looking for an authority figure, someone who would tell her exactly what she should do and feel. The problem with relying on the advice of an authority figure or an outside expert is that you never go beyond that person's experience to discover your own. You never gain a sense of your own authority. In psycho-physical rehearsal there is no right or wrong way to feel. Nobody outside of yourself can tell you what you should feel. The point is you should connect with your own way of being.

Another woman in a workshop said that during the walking exercise she felt like she was marching in an army. "I felt regimented; I didn't like it." Her dislike of the exercise may have been tied to her wearing of high-heeled shoes. But instead of letting her inner authority express the notion that she would be more comfortable if she kicked off her shoes, she forced herself to march in them. Because no one told her it was okay to take off her shoes, she felt she had to leave them on—no matter how hampered she felt in trying to do the exercise.

The psycho-physical rehearsal introduces you to your inner authority and teaches you to follow your own insights.

Walking Exercise Number 2

Walking exercise number two is a simulated walk over fire. You visualize in front of you a long pit of hot coals you are to walk over. You actually do stand up, but you do not move any parts of your body. You can visualize either yourself or your second self walking to the edge of the pit of hot coals.

Look into it. Feel the heat rising from it. You are barefoot and you are going to walk over this fire. Get ready. Go. Move at a speed that's comfortable for you. Walk all the way across. See yourself walking. Feel yourself walking across the coals. Go the entire length of the pit. Once you are at the other end, step out of the pit onto the ground.

Did you do it? Did you walk across the coals? If you did, can you tell me why? Did you take the walk because the instructions in this book told you to? Do you have to do as you're told to feel okay about yourself? Did you do as you were instructed because you felt that otherwise you would get no benefit from reading this book? Or because you would be ashamed to tell anyone you were afraid to visualize yourself walking over hot coals? Do you act only for the approval of others? Are your highest rewards from the approval of others? Do your major fears come from the disapproval of others? Does your desire for outside approval control the way you live?

As you can see from these questions, there is as much to consider in this second walking exercise as there is in any form of psycho-physical rehearsal. When you are answering these questions about why you did or did not walk across the hot coals, you will learn a great deal more about yourself if you use your paraconscious mind. If you let your conscious mind supply the answers, you may learn little or nothing. Remember, the conscious mind reacts only to those things that support its belief systems. Any answers you get from your conscious mind will confirm your pre-existing beliefs.

When you open your paraconscious mind to find answers, you will bypass and transcend the filters of doubt and fear that your conscious mind places over everything. To let your paraconscious mind work on the answers to the questions, ask them with your conscious mind and then turn your conscious mind off. Become an attentive observer. Do not try to think of answers. The answer will come. The point of this exercise is to teach you to use your paraconscious mind to discover your real options.

You know that you could have refused to walk across the fire. You could have said, "Hey, I'm not ready for that yet. I'm just a beginner." You had that option. You always have options. But you probably don't use them very often. You may not be aware of them because of your doubts and fears. Your self-esteem can also limit your awareness of the options available to you. With low self-esteem, you rely on outside authority for directions on how you should live your life. That authority does not always guide you in the ways that are best for you.

If you did take the walk across the fire pit, what was your motivation? Maybe you walked across the fire because you really wanted to have that experience. Your inner authority instructed you to take the steps, and you spontaneously obeyed. The two basic choices you have throughout your entire life are whether to do something because an outside authority has directed you to or to listen to and act on your own inner authority.

You do not need to follow the instructions in this book telling you to walk on fire. Neither do you need to listen to your conscious fears warning you not to walk on fire. Both of these voices are outside authorities. By using the autogenic psycho-physical rehearsal, you have the option of knowing what the universal mind and your own inner authority would recommend. Then you can follow that recommendation, regardless of whether it agrees with what I'm telling you in this book.

Go through the exercise again. Have your conscious mind create your vision of a fire pit and place you at the edge of it. Then turn off your conscious mind and observe. For most people, turning off the conscious mind is easier with the creation of a second self. Project your second self to the edge of the fire pit. Relax and watch. What you see your second self doing is entirely paraconscious mind input. The actions of your second self are informed by the universal mind. The emotions you are feeling and the thoughts you or your second self are thinking are also products of the paraconscious mind. They are true for you at this time. You are gaining the information you need to know how to act in the situation facing you. You are also adding to your personal power and resources.

Walking Exercise Number 3

The final walking exercise is a repeat of the first exercise. Instead of actually moving, however, you will do the exercise mentally. Many studies have shown that when you do an exercise mentally, you will experience it almost exactly as if you were doing it physically. When you visualize marching, you will know exactly how the motion feels in your legs, arms and body. Your body will undergo the same physiological changes during the visualization as it did when you were actually moving.

As you do this exercise, concentrate on the emotions and feelings involved. How excited are you and why? What do you feel in every part of your body? When you were marching in place, you did not have to think about how to do it. One leg goes up and comes down, then the other leg does the same. You have been familiar with that motion ever since you learned how to walk. It's automatic. No special concentration is required. During the visualization, once you set the marching in motion, the mechanics will take over. You will not have to think about the motion.

Begin this exercise by closing your eyes. You are going to march again, but without actually moving your body.

Mentally stand up.

Mentally march in place. Feel your legs going up and down. Note your emotions. What are you feeling as you march along?

Now step up your pace. March a bit faster. You are going toward a fantastic experience. Stay tuned in to your emotions. Let them run along with you.

Now march as fast as you can. Pick up your feet as rapidly as possible. Pump your arms. You are drawing closer to the place you want to be. Notice what you're feeling as you mentally move along at full speed.

Now slow back down to your original pace. Imagine you have spotted your destination. Feel that sense of impatience to get there. You're almost there. Right up ahead, that's where you're going. You are now moving very fast and excitedly. *Very* fast.

You have arrived. Slow down and enjoy this place you've been trying to reach for so long. Savor the moment.

But wait. They're calling you to return to the place you came from. You've got to go back. You'd better pick up the pace. Their calls seem urgent. You're excited to let them know what you've found on your trip. You have great stories to tell them. Go as fast as you can.

Okay. You're back. You can stop.

What happened? What did you experience? What did you experience in each part of your body? What did you feel? How excited were you and what excited you?

During this exercise one person said that she found herself making the trip on a camel. She did not set out to ride a camel during the exercise. But suddenly, there she was on one. She had stopped her conscious mind and opened her paraconscious mind, and a camel presented itself for her to ride. She felt all the movements of the camel, and the movements of her body. Her whole body chemistry changed with the experience of the camel.

The powerful fact you should have become aware of in these first exercises is that doing anything mentally is virtually equal to doing it physically. What an incredible option that gives you! How many things are there that you might like to do physically but that are not possible for you? With the autogenic psycho-physical rehearsal, there is no need to limit yourself. While sitting at home in Cleveland, I may wish to discover what I can learn from walking through a deep dark cave in Kentucky. I can use the autogenic psycho-physical rehearsal to do it.

You may want to know what it feels like to be in a bicycle race. Sit in your living room, close your eyes, turn off your conscious mind and live it. Your paraconscious mind will take you on a ride. You will be gathering intelligence from the universal mind all the while and adding to your wisdom and power.

You can use the autogenic psycho-physical rehearsal for all kinds of general self-improvement. Suppose you have a problem with nervousness when called on to give a speech. Even though you have no speeches scheduled, you can work on overcoming your public speaking jitters and understand where the nervousness comes from. By doing an autogenic psycho-physical rehearsal of your second self giving a speech and rehearsing until all your fears and doubts have been transcended and replaced by confidence, competence and excitement, you can get to the point where public speaking will be a joy rather than a chore.

Remember, to transcend means to replace anything less desirable with something more desirable. Some people call that magic. Some call it miracles. We call it normal. With applied active meditation we expect it.

With the autogenic psycho-physical rehearsal, you can create your own miracles daily. Each day you become more and more one with your creator.

The Swimming Exercise

For this psycho-physical rehearsal make sure you are comfortable. Sit down and begin to breathe from your diaphragm. Inhale quickly. Hold in. Exhale slowly. Count to at least sixteen when you exhale. That is the theta count. Breathe this way until you are in the rhythm of it.

Now set up your horizon. On your horizon project a beautiful swimming pool in a lush setting. By whatever route you prefer, move toward the swimming pool.

As you come closer to the swimming pool, notice the diving board. Then notice the slide. There are also steps leading into the pool. Allow your paraconscious to decide which entrance into the water you will choose. Your conscious mind is not participating in the choice. All the input is coming from your paraconscious.

Go into the water, using either the diving board, the slide or the steps—or whatever means of entry your paraconscious mind presents. Be fully aware of your surroundings. Note what the water feels like and what it smells like. What is the temperature of the air? What does the area around the pool look like?

Now find the most comfortable way to be in the pool. Your paraconscious mind will direct you to swim, float or perhaps stand in the shallow end. The choice is yours. Be open to whatever the paraconscious suggests and go with it. Stay in the pool for as long as you like, floating or swimming laps or treading water. Notice everything about the experience of being in the pool.

At some point, you may want to get out and choose another way of entering it, another way of being in it. Or maybe your paraconscious mind will direct you to do something else. Whatever suggests itself to you is input from the universal mind. Follow it. Glean all you can from the experience it is directing.

Be aware of your feelings and how your body is responding. Recognize the changes inside you. Open all your senses to the experience. You are a keen observer, and there is much to observe.

When you are ready, get out of the pool. Prepare to return to your conscious environment. Take several deep breaths as you return. Inhale and let go rapidly.

Pay attention to this so-called real world to which you have just returned. You have just come back from universal reality, which you might have previously called illusion. But since you have experienced universal reality, you may be more willing to accept its existence. You have experienced it in the physical sense and in the non-physical sense, i.e., in the universal sense.

I would like to explain why I chose this type of an experience for you. The way you did the exercise reveals a great deal about you. If a hundred different people do this exercise, it will be a hundred different exercises. Even though the instructions are the same for everyone, the way of following those instructions is unique to everyone. There is much symbolism in your way of doing the exercise. A symbol is packed with information. You can compare a symbol and its information to a computer command and the code attached to it. You type one command and an entire program runs. The one command calls up the totality of the program. Similarly, a symbol gives a set of instructions to your paraconscious and allows it to respond rapidly.

The symbol is not the truth but it keeps the mind on the truth. Think about what you experienced during the swimming pool exercise. Think about the symbolism of your behavior.

The swimming pool is a symbol for emotional capacity. If you swam one way at first and then tried a new, different style that felt more powerful, you released your attachment to the first method in order to increase your potential. The first way of swimming was easy and familiar. You discovered you wanted to move beyond the familiar. You put your energy into progressing, and you set free the power to expand your capabilities.

So now you see the options you have. You do not have to repeat only that which is familiar. Those old motions don't have any power over you any more. They will not help you develop your potential. When you respond spontaneously to something new, you can feel the energy and power.

How did the whole experience feel to you? Did you feel it in your body? Did you feel the movements of your arms and legs? Are you now convinced your muscles respond to your mental activity?

This psycho-physical rehearsal is one you can use again and again. You might have noticed some things that caused anxiety. For example, if you were afraid to dive, that is symbolic of the way you live your life. A fear of diving may indicate an unwillingness to take risks. If you do not dive, you probably have trouble being spontaneous. This diving is a test of your capacity to throw yourself unprepared into an activity.

Maybe you did try the dive, but you kept hitting your head on the bottom. This shows that diving at this time is not appropriate for you. Somehow it is a reaction rather than a response. You are still reacting to your fears if you hit your head. You cannot let go of these fears. When you transcend them, you will be able to dive. For now, you might do better to use the slide.

I am giving you these examples to show you how to use the psycho-physical rehearsal. Maybe for you, the swimming pool is not a symbol of emotional capacity. It may represent something else. Only you will know what. The point is to interpret all the symbols of the exercise. If the swimming pool does represent emotional capacity, you can use this exercise to gain insight into how to proceed in any situation involving the emotions. Then when you hit your head after diving in, you may know that your paraconscious mind is advising you to move cautiously in the situation. Where else but through a psycho-physical rehearsal can you obtain this invaluable knowledge about yourself and how you should respond? Where else can you develop your powers to their highest potential for your needs?

Your confidence in what the psycho-physical rehearsal has to tell you will increase as you continue to rehearse. Remember, it is a rehearsal. Keep rehearsing. Keep re-experiencing. You will gain awareness and power with each repeat rehearsal.

The Talk Show Exercise

This psycho-physical rehearsal can help you in many different aspects of your life. It deals particularly with your capacity to communicate what you are and to be freer and more open. This exercise can set your energy free. Prepare yourself for it. Sit erect and take your theta breaths, 4-4-16.

One problem to consider: the only thing that keeps you from becoming one with something or someone else is your ego. The ego wants to hold onto itself. It insists on separateness and individuality. It is vain about its own gorgeous form.

The creation of a second self can help you overcome the needs of your ego. Your paraconscious mind is free to give your second self any form. The form that your second self takes is important. It indicates that with which you wish to become one. It will take different forms depending on your wishes. It can adapt and change spontaneously. It is a flowing energy pattern not bound by a fixed shape. It has a great capacity for blending with other forms.

The creation of the second self is one of the most important techniques you can learn. Your second self bypasses your conscious mind and all the material you have stored in your subconscious mind. It is immediately in contact with your paraconscious mind and through it with the universal mind.

For the talk show host exercise, create a second self. This will set your energy free. Feel it go out. Observe what your paraconscious is showing you. You might discover some fascinating things about your paraconscious, about how your own universal mind perceives you.

Now set up your horizon; place your second self on that horizon. You remain outside the scene as an observer. Your second self is totally involved in the action you are observing. That second image is your eternal self, your thou self. It is your soul self getting involved.

Perhaps something is already appearing, some interaction going on between your second self and your horizon. Observe without trying to direct the action or make any changes.

Now on your horizon, create an image of your second self as a talk show host. Put this talk show host in an appropriate setting. Your second self may be making suggestions about where the host should sit or stand or what kind of furniture should be in the scene. Pay attention to these suggestions and follow them.

As soon as the environment seems settled and right, start inviting guests to appear on your talk show. Your conscious mind might choose the first guest. Or maybe your paraconscious mind is off and running so the conscious mind has no more work to do. Your guests are going to discuss a topic of your choice. Usually you will choose the topic before you begin this psycho-physical rehearsal. You use the rehearsal to focus on a particular issue which you want insight into. Sometimes, though, your paraconscious may present a topic.

The talk show host psycho-physical rehearsal borrows from Napoleon Hill's master mind concept. It lets you form your own master mind group any time you wish, lets you bring together whatever people you choose and adds the source of the greatest mind power in the universe, namely the universal mind. As the various guests appear and discuss the chosen topic, you will be both host and guest. You will act according to the instructions that your para-conscious mind is giving you. This is what the universal mind is directing you to do. Your subconscious mind is registering every part of this session, and the newly integrated information is being transmitted to your conscious mind so that the appropriate action can be taken.

The information, the people and the range of subjects have no limit during the show. Keep the talk show going for as long as your paraconscious wants it to run. Be the keenest of observers. You are not only the host and all the guests, but also the environment itself. Take note of everything and of all your feelings about everything. When the talk show is at an end, withdraw your second self from the horizon and allow it to re-enter and become part of your personal identity. Be aware of the feelings in your body. Note your emotions and thoughts.

Now take a deep breath. Release it with a sigh. When you feel you are alert enough, open your eyes. You have completed the psycho-physical rehearsal and are now in position to take appropriate action. And when you put it into action you have completed another circuit of self-empowerment for yourself.

Healing with the Autogenic Psycho-physical Rehearsal

An extremely important and exciting role of the autogenic psycho-physical rehearsal is helping you heal injuries and illnesses. With the autogenic psycho-physical rehearsal, you can shorten your healing time by as much as one-half. This is something everyone can do immediately. This alone will bring enough benefits to you to make all your efforts worthwhile.

Suppose you broke your leg. It's in a cast and the doctor has told you it will take six months to heal. Do an autogenic psycho-physical rehearsal. Pay no attention to the broken leg itself. Instead see yourself walking and running normally. Repeat the rehearsal numerous times, concentrating on normal activity of the injured part. Feel the increase in strength and excitement. This will dramatically reduce the time it takes your leg to heal.

Suppose you have a bad cold and cannot breathe through your nose. Do an autogenic psycho-physical rehearsal in which you feel yourself breathing freely and normally. Your body will get rid of the cold much faster. There is no limit to the uses you can make of this dramatic healing autogenic psycho-physical rehearsal.

After any psycho-physical rehearsal, you will be at a higher level of consciousness. It is important not to fall in love with and become attached to your new higher state of consciousness. Life on earth is a journey of evolution. Now that you have moved to this level, you should already be preparing new psycho-physical rehearsals and meditations that will move you to even higher levels. I once told my students that as my casket is being lowered into the ground, if they listen closely to my final vibrations, they will hear me saying, "I'm now leaving my attachment to earth and again I am moving on to a higher level."

The Sequence of Meditations

Learning the cosmic review and the psycho-physical rehearsals first is an important sequence and one you should follow if you want the program of applied active meditation to work for you. In *The Screwtape Letters* C.S. Lewis has Screwtape, who is a devil, instruct his nephew Wormwood in how to create destructive forces in a human being: "Keep his mind off the most elementary duties by directing it to the most advanced and spiritual ones." In other words, to ensure a person will not progress and that the person's life will become a hell, have him or her concentrate on highly spiritual values before getting the basics of life under control. Spiritual success requires great insight and power, which must be built through achievement in less lofty realms. Lewis is saying the path to spirituality requires developing sufficient wisdom and power to take care of earthly needs first. Only after you have the basics of physical existence under your control are you ready to move to higher levels.

The great humanistic psychologist Abraham Maslow made a science out of a similar observation. He describes five levels of needs, saying that an individual must satisfy the needs of the lower level before moving to the higher ones. Maslow's levels of needs in ascending order are: 1. physiological, 2. safety, 3. belonging, 4. esteem, and 5. self-actualization.

Before a person can move to a higher level, he or she must first develop the power and wisdom to achieve the needs of the lower level. Compare this to the development of a newborn child. First, the child learns to roll over. After the child has developed his or her ability to roll over, the ability to crawl is developed. The ability to roll over is not replaced, only added to by the ability to crawl. Next the child adds the ability to stand, then to walk and finally to run. In each instance the child develops to a higher level by adding skills to those he or she already has.

The cosmic review and psycho-physical rehearsals help you develop the powers to satisfy your basic needs. This is where you begin the process of self-empowerment. In doing the cosmic review and the psycho-physical rehearsals, you become acquainted with yourself, with your fears, doubts, hates and jealousies, your self-righteous thinking. You learn how to transcend these inappropriate thoughts and feelings, and add the wisdom and power needed for you to move to the next higher level.

When you do the cosmic review and psycho-physical rehearsals you will experience various problems. One or two will seem particularly important to you. Those that feel most important to you are the ones that apply to your most basic needs. They are the problems that you address first. When you have developed the power to transcend those, your most basic problems, then you are ready to move on to the next level.

The last two meditations—the guided and creative meditations—are different in their approach and in their objectives. The objectives of the cosmic review and psycho-physical rehearsals are more focused and therefore more limited. Their purpose is to achieve circuits of self-empowerment capable of handling your present needs and preparing you to move to higher needs.

The guided and creative meditations, on the other hand, are aimed primarily at achieving oneness with the universal mind and your creator. The purpose of the guided and creative meditations is the achievement of the deepest possible universal enlightenment.

As you do your guided and creative meditations you will find you are not a human being in search of a spiritual self. You are a spiritual being, an individualized divine self separated from the universal divine self. You are in search of further growth and becoming. And achieving that divine growth is a major purpose of our trip on earth.

When you truly recognize that you are an individualized divine self, you open yourself to great waves of inspiration that can transform your life completely. The more intensely you feel you are a divine self, the more intensely you will feel divine pride and the more profoundly you will experience freedom from all forms of limitations and dissatisfactions.

7
GUIDED MEDITATION

> *Does the Eagle know what is in the pit*
> *Or wilt thou go ask the Mole?*
> *Can Wisdom be put in a silver rod,*
> *Or Love in a golden bowl?*
> —William Blake, "The Book of Thel"

The Cosmic Review
and Psycho-physical Rehearsals

The cosmic review and psycho-physical rehearsals were the beginnings of your re-education. Through them, you learned about the universal mind and its application in everyday life. Understanding contact of the universal mind is a prerequisite for moving on to the broader levels of meditation. The meditations done to date have prepared us for the guided and creative meditations we will now do. However, these meditations do not replace the cosmic review and psycho-physical rehearsals. They add a new dimension. For our daily lives and its problems and desires we will continue to use the cosmic review and psycho-physical rehearsals.

In addition, when you have anything troubling you, before undertaking a guided or creative meditation, it helps to first cleanse yourself of your troubles with the cosmic review and/or psycho-physical rehearsals.

When you get into the habit of cleaning out destructive feelings daily, you will have to devote less and less time to this form of housekeeping. You can compare it to washing dirty dishes after a meal. If you wait a week to wash the dishes you will have a great deal to do. When you do it immediately after each meal, there is

98

little to do. Once your mind is empty of negatives, you will need less sleep and perhaps less food, you will be healthier, and you will be much more aware and powerful.

The Guided Meditation

Guided meditation uses the conscious mind far differently than our accustomed usage. In guided meditation we use our conscious mind to create a fantasy. The conscious mind functions we've used so far were, in various degrees, related to reality—related to our "real" life. In the guided meditation we remove our conscious mind from our life and move it into fantasy. Doing so minimizes its attachments and belief systems. It deactivates many of the physiological attachments and neurotransmitter communications in our nervous system.

Guided meditation is a short conscious mind fantasy that brings to us a unique conscious mind input. The conscious mind input we have so far used is related to limited and specific areas of our life. It therefore communicates predominantly with specific and limited areas of the universal mind.

On the other hand, the guided meditation coming from conscious fantasy allows for a very generalized communication with the universal mind and brings to us a deep and generalized inflow of universal intelligence not otherwise available. It is a very broad inflow of universal intelligence applying to almost all areas of our life and is useable almost continually. It fits our description of enlightenment as a generalized increase in personal powers coupled with the achievement of higher knowledge.

Thus the conscious mind inflow of information from the guided meditation is unique. For that reason, as you will see, the universal intelligence we receive from it is also unique.

Becoming Whole

With the transformations that occur through the guided and creative meditations you will feel a wholeness not available in any other way. A number of things will come together.

1. All three parts of the mind (conscious, subconscious, paraconscious) are operating in total harmony. Neither the input from the conscious mind nor the paraconscious is turned off. They work alternately and in complete harmony.

2. You have the deepest possible interaction with your universal creative force, and you are discovering that you and your creative force are one.

3. You feel and know you are one with everything in the universe.

The guided and creative meditations can be compared to the cosmic review and psycho-physical rehearsals just as the world news can be compared to the local news. As we learn the guided and creative meditations we open ourselves to a much greater inflow, a much more complete source of information.

You Have All the Answers

What is important to know at all times is that the answers lie *within you*! Nowhere else. They lie within your use of your total mind. And you need to express those answers according to the way *you* have experienced life and not by the way others have, or told you the way you should have. My truth is never going to be your truth and vice versa.

And my truth is not static for me. It changes continually. It is not, *the* truth. I can never say, "This is the way it is." I can always say, "This is the way it is for me, and I share this with you. Now let's see what it becomes for you." In that way we don't infringe on other people's individual essences.

Meditation gives us insight into how we perceive life and how we need to act upon our perceptions. And it gives us the power to act successfully. Meditation is more than a tool. It is not only a life process; it is *the* process of living. When I am asked, "When do you meditate," I have to answer, "Almost every waking hour." All day long I am perceiving my paraconscious input and acting upon it. I am also continually aware of my conscious mind input and my paraconscious response to it. Thus I constantly have a very strong perception of what is happening beyond my own individual essence and I'm able to respond. That's what I mean when I use the phrase, "applied active meditation." Meditation is, as you will see, applied continually. When you become proficient, you will find yourself living applied active meditation all day long, every day.

In the guided meditation, we respond to a consciously created fantasy. During the entire meditation we are open to the input of the conscious mind. However, without any direction by us or our second self, the paraconscious input will enter throughout the meditation. This gives us the chance to respond to both, and to be aware of the interaction between them.

Many times throughout the meditation we will experience the result of this combination. The guided meditation is unique in offering this. We experience in sequence the conscious mind input, the paraconscious response to it, and the action it leads to. No other meditation offers us such a feast.

When you are first learning applied active meditation, you should follow certain prescribed steps. Eventually, you will have gone through those steps often enough that you will no longer need them. When that occurs you will find you are responding to each day of your life as if it were a guided meditation. The moment you're confronted with a situation, you will use your total mind, just as you will learn to do in the guided meditation. You will become immediately aware of the input of your conscious mind and then the absolute power being brought to you by your paraconscious. And when you respond, you will be putting that power into action.

The Guided Meditation Process

Guided meditation is a prelude to creative meditation, which is the topic of the next chapter. Creative meditation works on themes and ideas. In guided meditation, you discover what themes and ideas are most important and most powerful for you.

The guided meditation is inaugurated by, and then directed by, the conscious mind. In the guided meditation the conscious mind plays an important and usually continuing part. It begins with a script prepared by the conscious mind.

The purpose of the guided meditation is to create a situation in which the universal mind will present us with a theme or idea that we can meditate on, and that will lead us to the highest knowledge and power available to us. At the end of the guided meditation we are presented with a theme, idea or image. We then use this as the subject for our creative meditation.

The conscious mind prepares a script for the meditation. Your second self is the main actor in the script. Your conscious mind then directs the actions of your second self and of the entire script. However, almost invariably, as you go through the script it will change. Non-script events will begin to take place. In some instances a completely new script may take form. Since these changes are not directed by the conscious mind, they are from the paraconscious mind and universal intelligence.

Because your conscious mind is so active, you may encounter some fears and anxieties. Your paraconscious mind will be functioning also, and you will have the opportunity of being aware of both the input from it and from your conscious mind. For each conscious fear you become aware of, you will get a paraconscious vision with which to replace it. Very often, as the guided meditation goes on, the paraconscious input becomes stronger.

At the conclusion of a guided meditation, you will be aware of a theme. This theme is important for you and is one that will bring you great rewards in the creative meditation. The theme comes from your paraconscious, which draws it out from all the ideas in the guided meditation. This theme will give you the deepest penetration into the universal mind and, hence, the greatest enlightenment.

Guided meditation puts you in touch not only with generalized universal intelligence, but also with your own higher creative force. In the guided meditation both your conscious and your paraconscious minds are active. Immediately after you begin your guided meditation with the script from your conscious mind, you go into a theta (4-8-16) or delta (4-8-32) breathing pattern. You become aware of the interactions taking place between your conscious and your paraconscious minds.

At the conclusion of your guided meditation you will completely empty your mind. It will become a void, "the silence beyond all sound." Into this void your paraconscious mind will bring a theme. This will be the theme for your creative meditation.

The Process

The guided meditation begins with a conscious mind script. You can also choose an object or event to serve as a script. To begin the guided meditation, create a three-dimensional scene outside of yourself. The scene is always outside and never in your head. Then create a second image of yourself. This image enters the scene and becomes a part of it. You remain an observer and never enter into the scene. You remain very concerned, very involved, but outside of and therefore non-attached to the scene. As usual, you are breathing in theta or delta.

In guided meditation you project and experience the script of the meditation as if you were seeing a movie. You send your second self into the scene. Your conscious mind will initially direct both your second self and the scene. As your second self enters the scene, changes usually occur that your conscious mind did not direct. Do not allow your conscious mind to interfere with these spontaneous changes. Let the scene change and flow. These changes are your paraconscious mind expressing itself.

Observe the vision, the wisdom and power the paraconscious mind is adding to the events of the script. Experience it mentally, physically and emotionally. But remain non-attached leaving your energy free to flow.

In guided meditation, you can consciously change the scene any time you wish. You can consciously add any emotions and acts to see how the universal mind will respond to them. However, changes will be occurring not related to your conscious mind. They are from the paraconscious. Do nothing to stop or change this input. Flow with it.

Pick A Quiet Place First

To do your first guided meditations, I suggest you choose a place where you will not be disturbed. Keep in mind that this is a means to an end. As you become proficient, you will be doing guided meditations any time during the day that you wish. Choose a room that will be quiet. Adjust the lighting so it is soothing and comfortable.

You can sit on the floor on a blanket, a firm cushion or pillow. Or you can sit in a chair. If you choose a chair, make sure it is low enough for your feet to be flat on the floor. Wear loose fitting, ordinary clothing that does not restrict your posture or breathing.

Sit with your back straight. Breathe deeply. Go into the theta or delta breathing rhythm. Once your theta breathing is automatic, fix your gaze on an imaginary point directly in front of you, about ten feet away.

Meditation on Objects

It is usually best to begin your practice of guided meditation with simple objects. Choose a common physical object that you can easily visualize: a dinner plate for example. You will use the meditation to discover everything about that plate: What does it look like? What design is on it? Does the design have meaning? Do you have any feelings associated with the plate? Do you feel hungry when you see it? Is there any odor involved? What does the plate feel like? What do you plan for this dish? How will it enter into your life? What paraconscious input are you receiving in response to your feelings?

Once you are capable of finding a theme in a common physical object like a dinner plate, it is simple to find a theme in anything, from daily experiences to abstract ideas. You can also integrate into your guided meditation things that are negative to you, unpleasant things you have never—and would rather not—experience. Isn't it better to become acquainted with them in meditation than in real life? Then if they or other similar negative experiences happen to you, you will have increased your inner power and resources so you can transcend them.

Remember to transcend means you have the power and wisdom to replace the negative event with a positive one. Therefore nothing you have the power to transcend can ever harm you! With the powers you have added to yourself by the meditations, when negative events occur, rather than harming you, they become stepping stones to a new transcendence that increases your personal power. If the difficult experiences of your fantasy meditations never do happen, you still have been able them to build your own personal power. And you have used them without having to actually live through the pain of experiencing them.

The Formal Steps

Guided meditation has seven steps: concentration, decentralization, creation of the second self, penetration, contemplation, synthesis and erasure.

Step 1. Concentration

The first step is to concentrate on an object, a script, an event or an idea. Create a three-dimensional image of whatever scene you will be thinking about. The image is always in front of you and never in your head. Visualize the image in every detail: size, form, colors, texture, sound, smell, taste, etc.

Step 2. Decentralization

Once you have focused on your object, decentralize from everything else. Become aware of nothing other than the scene of your meditation. The image completely fills your mind as if it were engraved there. Avoid any conscious mind questioning, doubting or speculation.

Step 3. Create your second self

As soon as you have concentrated on your object and decentralized from all else, create the image of your second self. See your second self walk away from you and approach the object.

At this point, or any other time during the meditation, a stray thought may intervene and interfere with your concentration. Do not in any way focus on or fight this thought. To the extent you pay attention to it or fight it, you become attached to it. When you become attached to it, you block your flow of energy. You make the interference stronger by feeding it your energy.

Remain unattached by allowing it to flow by uninterrupted, as if you were watching a train. When the stray thoughts stop, the train has passed. Cross the tracks, and observe your second self begin to interact with the scene you have created.

Step 4. Penetration

Direct your second self to enter into and interact with the scene you are observing. Your second self will interact with both the conscious mind input and any paraconscious mind inflow. It penetrates the entire scene. You may consciously alter the scene at any time and in any way you wish. Add any emotions you wish to observe or actions you wish to experience. By so doing you empower yourself to transcend them! Each time *you* change the scene, you are gaining access to the universal mind that is the opposite pole from what you have consciously added. By the action of the meditation the two poles are connected and the flow of energy created is very powerful!

Step 5. Contemplation

Contemplation begins at this point. Your conscious mind becomes an observer. You perceive and experience clearly what is arising from your paraconscious mind. You do not have to have your inflow of universal intelligence verified by anyone else or any outside authority. You accept the information from universal intelligence exactly as you received it. In the guided meditation you can then immediately put it to use and experience what it can do for you. Knowledge and truth never come to you from outside sources. They come only from what you experience.

Step 6. Synthesis

In this step you put it all together. You review all that has occurred during the meditation. You have had many experiences. Now is the time to put all the details together into a full picture, to see the totality. To accomplish this, you mentally surround the scene with energy so it becomes a totality. The energy can be in the form of a white light, a cocoon, or whatever your paraconscious brings you. Your paraconscious mind will suggest an image that works for you. Use that image to fuse the scene. For me, in almost every guided meditation, I surround the scene with a very bright white light. The white light not only surrounds the scene, it penetrates every part of it.

Some people get a theme or idea at this point in the meditation. This will be the subject for their creative meditation. I rarely experience the theme during the synthesis. The theme for my creative meditation usually comes during the erasure step. If you experience the theme during synthesis, then use the erasure step only to prepare for a creative meditation.

Step 7. Erasure

The energy now becomes so bright, so powerful it melts the scene in front of you. As the scene melts, it is transformed into energy itself. Take a last look and let it go. If anything still remains, consciously erase it. See only the white emptiness before you. Into this emptiness, the universal mind will deposit a theme or idea. This is the subject for your creative meditation.

Sample Exercises

These sample exercises are rather involved, just as your life is. They contain much symbolism. I offer them here to show you how you might consciously choose a story or a scenario upon which to meditate. These exercises are favorites among people taking Jack Schwarz's workshops. There are more exercises in his book, *Voluntary Controls*. They are fertile ground for conscious and paraconscious mind interactions.

If you do not have someone to read these exercises to you, tape-record them and then play them to guide you through. Remember, the object is to use these exercises and the applied active meditation process to give you the power at all times to communicate with the universal mind and have it as an integral and ongoing part of your life.

Guided Meditation Number 1:
The Clay Statue

Sit erect. Breathe deeply, preferably in theta or delta.

Create in front of you, with eyes open or closed as you prefer, a horizon. Between your horizon and yourself let there be the image of a green meadow. It is a very beautiful lush grass meadow. See this meadow with your whole being. Smell the grass. Feel the coolness of the blades. Breathe in the fresh air. Feel the breeze. Experience the total environment. Use all your senses.

At the edge of the meadow, there is a body of water. It could be a pool, a stream, a lake or even an ocean. And close to the water is a pile of clay.

Focus on this entire scene—the meadow, the body of water, the clay. Notice everything about it. What do you smell? What do you see? What do you taste? What do you hear? What do you feel? Close out everything but the scene.

Now create your second self. Have that second self walk toward the pile of clay. Observe how your second self is interacting with the scene. Gather more and more information about the environment.

Your second self is approaching the pile of clay. Now your second self is touching the clay, picking up handfuls and mixing them with the water. Your second self begins kneading the clay and forming it into something. Sense the texture of the clay. Feel the water flowing through your hands. Feel the muscles in your hands as your second self kneads the clay. Notice the shape the clay is taking.

Your second self is creating a statue of you. This statue is formed in the most beautiful way you can imagine. It is a perfect being. Its substance is total creativity. Watch as your second self works away on getting this clay sculpture just right. Look at the work from all angles. Observe every movement that your second self makes.

When the sculpture is finished, allow your second self to stand back and look at it. Without prejudice or bias—with pure perception only—observe the statue. Direct your second self to make any alterations, adding or removing clay, cutting, re-kneading, etc.

Watch carefully and objectively as your second self makes changes in the sculpture. What is being trimmed away? What is being added? Observe all the changes. When the work appears to be complete, place a bright fire on the horizon close to the statue. Have your second self put the statue into the fire to bake it. Feel the heat of the flames. See the color of the light they cast. Notice everything you can as you watch this kiln process.

Now the flames are dying down and disappearing. Feel the breeze. The air is cooling the sculpture. Study the finished sculpture. After its firing, how does it differ from its first form? Note any similarities and any differences between you, your second self and the statue of yourself. What do you feel? What thoughts are flowing freely through your mind?

When you have thoroughly absorbed the feedback from this scene and the statue, merge the statue with your second self. Surround both the statue and your second self with brilliant white light. The light is fusing the statue with your second self. Allow your second self to incorporate all of the statue's qualities you observed. Then direct your second self to return to you and to integrate all of its properties with you. Wrap yourself and your second self with white light. Feel the light's fusing power.

This is your rebirth. You have just had the opportunity to redo yourself, to add all the qualities you always have desired. And by merging your second self with your physical self, you thereby can experience a total renewal of being. The you of your past experiences has died. A new you has been born at a higher level of consciousness.

The white light is now growing even more brilliant. It is so bright it is blotting out the scene from which your renewed second self emerged. Into this void, the paraconscious mind will bring a theme. The guided meditation is at an end.

The clay statue meditation is one that you can go through again and again. Your paraconscious will reveal new information to you each time. And you will be able to re-experience the qualities of your statue at any given time, at any given place, and to make changes.

Follow Your Own Imagination

Be attentive to all aspects of your guided meditation, including the unusual and often fleeting ones. Do not be concerned if at some point you go off into a self-centered adventure and leave behind the voice that is reading the meditation's instructions to you. As long as you maintain your perspective as a spectator watching your second self and calmly monitoring what happens, you will reap the rewards of your meditation. Follow your imagination and you will produce scenarios that are especially meaningful for you.

As you use guided meditations, you will notice the evolution of your experiences from ordinary three-dimensional scenes toward ineffable, almost indescribable experiences. At first you will be able to identify yourself within the meditations and note the specific actions and feelings they illicit from you.

However, sooner or later you will find it difficult to express your experiences accurately. Being unable to express your experiences accurately does not mean you can't make use of them. On the contrary. Their inexpressible nature indicates you have absorbed their significance so deep within you, so thoroughly and in such a diffused fashion, that they are beyond our everyday language.

You will know certain values and realities about yourself and the world that cannot be verified by logic or suitably rendered in words. Your intuitive capacity, your communication with the universal mind, cannot be intellectualized and still remain vital. To communicate indescribable experiences, you will have to resort to the same mode through which you received them—symbols and metaphors.

This sort of experience is very personal. That is why symbols and metaphors cannot be effectively borrowed from others. You must have your own which have individual meaning for you. Just follow your heart and take responsibility for shaping your methods of communication with the universal mind. You will recognize your own experiences as you go through self-discovery. Once you recognize them, you must accept them as your own. This acceptance will result in the development of your own unique process for converting intelligence from the universal mind into personal power.

Guided Meditation Number 2:
The Mountain Exercise

Sit erect in a chair with head, neck and body aligned. Take three alpha breaths (8-8-8-4), then one alpha-theta (4-8-8-4), one theta (4-8-16-4), and one delta (4-8-32-4).

Now set up your horizon with a hilly area. The sun is shining in a bright blue sky. Between you and the horizon, you see a marvelous, lush grassy meadow. Concentrate on the grass. Smell it. Touch it. Your feet are bare, and you're walking across this meadow. How does the grass feel? Is it cool or has it been warmed by the sun?

Create your second self and send that image out into the meadow. You may suddenly perceive something more than just grass. Note whatever it is. Do not try to influence what you see. Tune into all the sounds of the environment.

Now direct your second self to start moving in any specific way that you want—running, walking, dancing—any kind of motion will get your second self to the horizon. Experience that motion.

Your second self is approaching the horizon. You can feel the excitement your second self feels. Your second self is the main participant in this scene. You are an observer.

Your second self arrives at the foot of a mountain, which is surrounded by impenetrable brush. Your conscious mind sees no way through the bush. If there is a way through your paraconscious mind will know how to find it. Your goal is to get past the brush so you can begin climbing the mountain. Let your paraconscious mind lead you to an opening in the brush. Or if there's not an opening, maybe there's another way through. Pay attention to input from your paraconscious. It will lead you through the brush.

Once you find your way past the brush, you are on a path covered with huge rocks. These boulders are the next obstacle. You need to find a way to get past them. Allow your paraconscious mind to direct you. Watch as your second self moves up the mountain, guided by the universal mind.

Your second self climbs until you reach the first summit of the mountain. This is the place where all the animals of the world gather. They are all waiting for you on the mountain. Your second self responds to the presence of all these creatures. Observe the interaction of your second self with the animals of the world. Notice everything.

But the summit where all the animals are is not your destination. You must move on to the next summit. Your second self must move through a sea of animals to find the path again. Use all of your senses to experience this motion. Notice the feelings your second self has. Notice the thoughts. Keep moving through the animals and up the mountain.

As you get closer to the next summit, your excitement and sense of anticipation increase. This climb is one you've been wanting to do for a long time. Once you arrive at the second summit, you notice a huge building. This building blocks the trail up the mountain. If you are to continue on, you must go through the building. Follow the input of your paraconscious mind to find your way into and through the building. As you enter, notice the doors. Pay attention to the smell of the building and how it contrasts with the mountain air you've been breathing. How does it feel to be inside the building? What do you see? What do you hear? What do you taste? Can you touch the walls? What is the floor made of? What are your emotions as you pass through the building?

Leave the building through the rear doors. You are now on the trail again and ascending. You are headed to the top of the mountain. You are up so high you're in the clouds. You are having difficulty seeing because they are so thick. You don't know, if you are on a narrow trail or a wide one. All you can do is watch yourself place one foot in front of the other and trust you will make the right moves. Your paraconscious mind is guiding your steps. Play close attention to the information it is giving you.

You climb and climb. Suddenly you emerge from the clouds. You feel the warm sun. You have reached the top of the mountain, and the view is fantastic. You can see forever in all directions. You turn in a circle, taking everything in. You can see what lies ahead of you. You can look back and see the experiences you've already been through. Your level of awareness has expanded significantly.

Savor the feelings at the top of the mountain. You have raised your level of consciousness by ascending. You can sense the dramatic increase in your excitement and your sense of freedom. You have a much broader sense of the world.

When you have taken in the view from the top, begin the climb back down. As you are descending, you will pass others who are on the journey you just made. These others are struggling to get to the top. Share your experience with them.

As you go back down the trail, notice any changes in the scenery. Are the clouds just below the peak still thick? When you reach the level where the building blocks the path, is it the same building? Is the interior different? What else do you notice at this level? And when you reach the first summit, the one where all the animals of the world were gathered, see if any changes have taken place. Are all the animals still there? Which ones do you see? Are you interacting any differently? What is happening around you?

Proceed down the mountain. You will encounter the boulders again. Or maybe the path is clear this time. What has happened to that section of the trail? And once you reach the base of the mountain, is the brush still an obstacle? Do you find your way through the brush immediately? On the other side of the brush is the grassy, lush meadow. Let your second self enjoy standing in it. Look around that meadow. Is it any different from the way you saw it before you ascended the mountain?

Use the white light to help you absorb all the information you can. Surround your second self and yourself with the light and pull your second self toward you. Fuse your second self with your body. Sense what has happened to you.

Expand the light to cover the scene. Increase its brightness until you can see nothing but the light. Now into this void will come an idea or a theme from the universal mind. Take a deep breath and release it with a sigh. Once more, breath deep, and release it with a sigh. Come back into your conscious awareness.

The guided meditation to the mountain top has several ingredients. These are of an evolutionary nature, designed to activate what you need to deal with. The purpose of the meditation goes beyond being a nice experience for you. It is more than taking a walk on a beautiful mountain path and enjoying nature. It reveals a theme of great significance to you.

I will tell you the symbolism that each of the ingredients in the meditation has for me. You may interpret a symbol differently. That's fine. Only *you* can know what each piece of the meditation means.

For me, the meadow is a symbol of growth. It is green and lush. The grasses are swaying gently and are in constant motion because of the breeze. The brush at the base of the mountain symbolizes obstacles to the achievement of my objectives and desires. It represents mental as well as physical barriers. These are barriers of my own making. The important thing is to find a way through the brush. Sometimes students tell me they are totally stuck in the brush and unable to find an opening. Then I know how they view their lives. They don't see a way to grow. They think change is impossible.

When your paraconscious mind takes over, however, you will find your way through the brush. The universal mind will lead you to the path up the mountainside. You will see how clever and powerful the universal mind is. The universal mind that guides your way through the brush becomes a permanent part of you. It will be there for your use whenever you encounter obstacles to your goals.

After the brush, you come upon rocks. These are more obstacles. Every time you think you have a clear path, there is another barrier to overcome. These constant obstacles help you grow. They teach you to rely on your paraconscious mind and to take direction from the universal mind. By gathering the universal intelligence needed to find a clearing through the brush and to move over the boulders, you are taking control of your life. You are applying universal intelligence in your daily routine.

Let's say you have an important business meeting. You are the only one who arrives on time; everyone else is twenty minutes late. Not only are they late, they are also in no mood to agree with your ideas. They start to pick apart what you are saying. They begin to pull you down. They are the rocks in your path. If you react to your frustration you give power to your frustration. Instead you respond by turning to a higher need.

Your universal intelligence inflow will give you an image of that higher need. It will also show you the actions to take to achieve that higher need. You replace your frustration with the *action* needed to achieve that higher need. Whereas before you reacted to those who disagreed with you, now you can respond to what the universal mind is telling you to do. And with each such response you add to your personal power and wisdom.

The animals at the first summit are symbolic of your animal nature. Your interaction with these animals can tell you a great deal about how you perceive yourself in the physical world. Did you move comfortably here? Were there some animals that you hoped would not be here? Which were they? And what do they mean to you? If there is an animal that frightens you and you see it at this level of the mountain, you can consciously give yourself directions to go to that animal and pet it. Be with that animal until you feel the fear going away. Sometimes you will not have to do this consciously. You will head toward a ferocious animal and feel terror. Then you may be working out generalized fears. Go toward that which makes you afraid. Use your fear as a spur to action.

If you did not see any animals at this first summit, that's okay. Trust your paraconscious! The instructions I'm giving you are merely a map. Your paraconscious knows the territory better than any map I could design. It is the walker of the path and the pioneer of your frontiers. Pay attention to it. Do not try to see something that your paraconscious does not readily make visible. If you didn't encounter any animals at the first summit, your paraconscious knew that your physical nature is not an issue with you. You do not have to deal with it now. Take what your paraconscious has to show you and work to understand that.

At the second summit, the type of building you encounter has significance. I did not specify a type when I gave you the meditation. I didn't say that a shed was blocking your path. Nor did I identify the building as a palace or temple or church. What kind of building did you see? Whatever type it was, the suggestion came from the universal mind via your paraconscious mind. You needed to experience that type of building. Figure out the significance of that building.

Did you feel peaceful once you were inside the building? Or were you ill at ease? The inside of the building symbolizes your heart. The

Sufis say, "As long as there is room in your heart for one foe, it is a very unsafe abode for a friend." A foe can be any inappropriate thought or feeling, which is to say, anything that blocks your awareness and keeps you from growing. A friend coming into your heart will not be safe as long as even one foe is there. Your appropriate thoughts can find no place to lodge because of the presence of inappropriate thoughts. You may have envy in your heart. Or resentment. Or hate. There is room then for nothing else. One little toxin in your heart can make your whole body toxic.

In the building that symbolizes your heart, you must observe how safe you feel. Did you hear any sounds when you were in the building? Students have said they heard bells ringing or water running. In the building, I experience a release from myself. I feel enriched. I smell roses and hear the love music of Sigmund Romberg. I experience myself merging with a person or with people I love. That merger creates a new entity, which then becomes one with my creator. Empowered and excited, I am ready, even anxious, to move on.

The final summit of the mountain is the peak, the crown. You may reach this level, but do not be content with it. Too many people have one peak experience and spend the rest of their lives talking about it. They never realize their peak was just a low mountain and that many other mountains are much higher. The peak is never a stopping place. It is always a springboard for the next mountain. People who get attached to one peak experience are stuck. When you choose to live the process rather than being results-oriented, one peak will lead to another and another and another. You will have tremendous momentum and will always be moving to higher levels.

I always have a specific feeling each time I meditate. I come out of the meditation feeling excited and radiant. I may not remember exactly what happened or be able to talk about the experience, but I know it was great. It was a peak experience.

The next time I meditate, if I begin from scratch looking for the same feeling, I will go nowhere new. I will not increase my power and wisdom. Instead, I use my state of excitement, the radiance I felt after my last meditation, as the starting point for my new meditation. I want to begin each new meditation as close as possible to the peak I reached during my last meditation. I try to be aware of the total meditation process without getting attached to the results of one exercise. I do not say I wanted this or that out of meditation and because I got what I wanted I have arrived. By using my last peak experience as a baseline, I am constantly growing and evolving. I will never arrive. Why would I want to stop this glorious process?

For any meditation to add power to you, you must experience it at a high voltage. This power comes to you when you raise your excitement level as the meditation begins and progresses. If a meditation does not excite you, if you do not feel exhilarated by taking control of your life and experiencing what you desire, you will not get much out of that particular meditation. Your excitement level will go sky high when you share your life with your creator and your creative energy. You will know by your excitement level if the meditation is working.

If you doubt your excitement level is important, try this experiment. The next time you have a meeting with other people, decide that nothing is going to go right. When you are in the meeting room, think of all the reasons why it is an unpleasant place to be. Pick one person, and decide you don't like him. Think of all the other things you would rather be doing. You will feel your energy drop to zero. You will be totally ineffective at your meeting. You might as well be anywhere else. The same holds true for meditation if your excitement level does not rise.

Guided Meditation Number 3: River and Cavern Exercise

Sit erect on a chair. Align your head and neck with your spine. Your eyes can be open or closed. Breathe in a theta or delta rhythm.

Project your horizon. Imagine a second self. Consciously create a swift-flowing river through the center of a lush green meadow. Imagine the river to be flowing away from you toward the horizon. Your second self is standing at the river's edge, watching the water foam and bubble. The banks of the river are covered with soft, springy vegetation, and your second self strolls barefoot along the river's edge. Feel the earth beneath your feet. Open your pores and sense the activity of the nerve endings in your feet. You feel revitalized and energized. Far down the river, your second self encounters a cave. Settle down near the cave and quietly contemplate it.

Eventually, someone or something will come out of the cave, awakened by your attention. Allow your second self to interact with it and check all your reactions to it without changing, evaluating, judging or interpreting those reactions. Remember what has come out of the cave. It will be an excellent theme for a creative meditation.

Notice that one entrance to the cave particularly attracts you. Move your second self through this entrance. You are in darkness. Feel the rough texture of the stone walls and the coolness of the air.

Be aware of everything you feel and what you sense. Be present in the cave. Walk through the passageway until you reach a cavern. You will find other beings there. Stay with them. Interact with them. Mentally record your actions and responses.

Leave the cavern and move on through the passageway until you come to an opening into the outside world. What do you find when you walk out into the open? Do you feel warmth and sunshine? Or is the day overcast? Note all the details of the environment into which you emerge. Experience it fully and then go back into the cave. Retrace your route, entering the cavern again and responding to the beings you find there. Once you leave the cave the second time, walk along the riverbank.

As your second self moves toward you, wrap it and yourself together in white light. Increase the intensity of that light so your second self melts into you. Then expand the light to obliterate the scene from which your second self emerged. Take note of the theme that the universal mind is bringing for your creative meditation.

Take three deep breaths and release them with a sigh. Record all your experiences in your journal. This time figure out the symbolism for yourself. What did the river mean for you? The cavern? What about any animal you encountered?

Guided Meditation Number 4: The Cube and Sphere

Again sit erect, aligning your head, neck and spine. Breathe rhythmically in theta or delta. Project your horizon, laying out the lush meadow. Create your second self on the horizon.

Imagine a blue cubicle and your second self floating up to it and circling it until you are fully aware of its three dimensions. Direct your second self to enter the cubicle and expand its energy to light the interior. When there is enough light, you can see you are in a square room. There is someone—or something—else also in the room. Do not consciously create this occupant, but know you resent and dislike it very much. Let your second self interact with it, and note all the changes, physiological and emotional.

When you are finished interacting with this hated being or thing, you notice a door in the cubicle that leads to another room. Enter this room, which is brightly lit and circular. Someone or something you love very much is waiting there for you. Do not consciously choose what you find here. Interact with this loved being or thing until you feel you have played the scene out. Mentally record the feedback as you did before.

Next open the door between the two rooms. Pull the occupant of the square room into the round room. Watch as your second self interacts with both. Carefully notice all that is happening. When you are finished, leave the cubicle and float back to the meadow. Create a wrap of light around yourself and your second self so the two fuse. Then expand the light and increase its brilliance until it has erased all traces of the scene. Be aware of the theme that comes into the void. Take three deep breaths and release with a sigh. Record your experience in your journal, once again noting the meaning that all the parts of the meditation had for you.

Guided Meditation Number 5:
The Seven Door Exercise

Sit erect, with your head, neck and spine aligned. Breathe in a theta or delta rhythm. Close your eyes if you like. Project your horizon, including the lush meadow.

Imagine your second self moving through the meadow toward the horizon. Be aware of any sounds, smells, feelings and sights along the way. When you reach a slope, you will see a three-story building. Direct your second self to approach the building, entering through the double doors you find there. Walk down three steps, through a portal and into a long corridor. There are seven doors on the right side of the corridor and seven on the left. All are different colors. Note the color of each.

Walk down the corridor and choose a door on the right that you wish to open. Does the door have a label on it? If so, note what it says. Then enter the space behind that door. Do not change anything about the space; simply observe what is being shown to you. What is there and what kind of feedback are you getting? What does your second self look like? What physical sensations do you feel? What is the general atmosphere within the space? What impresses you the most? What changes are taking place? Remember what you find in this space because, later on, you can always go back into it and make conscious changes. As you leave, close the door, but do not lock it.

Next choose a door on the left side of the corridor. Check to see if it has a label and, if so, remember it. Open the door and enter the space. Investigate it. Be a good investigator; become very observant of all you can discover within the space. After you have done this, leave the space and do not lock the door. You want to be able to re-enter it whenever you wish. Now slowly walk down the corridor and enter any doors you wish on either side. Check the labels on any door you enter, and mentally record the entire experience.

Finally you reach the farthest end of the corridor. Here is a force field that, at this moment, acts like a mirror. You are confronted with a mirror image of your second self. Observe it. Take note of all the differences among your three selves. After you have done this, realize this is a force field you can move through. Move through it, constantly observing and recording all feedback, all experiences.

Beyond the force field is a large circular space with a soft, clay-like dirt floor. There is no ceiling. Walk straight to the middle of the space. Realize you are moving from the south to the north side. Somewhere in this space, buried a couple of inches below the soft floor, a book is hidden. As you stand in the middle of the space, become aware of the presence and the location of the book. Go to it and dig it up. Remember in which direction you moved: west, northwest, east, south, southeast or whatever. When you have found the book, notice it is an ancient picture book. Open it and page through it. If any specific picture attracts you, gaze upon it for some moments and record within your mind what it shows you. Then replace the book and realize you can find it again at any time.

Return to the center of the space and walk south, back to the entrance of the space, the force field. Leave the circular space through this field and turn to observe yourself in the mirror once you are again in the corridor. Again, observe any changes that have taken place. When you have done so, turn to look at the doors on the left and right and see if everything is as you left it. Leave the same way you came, up three steps, out the double doors and back into the meadow. With your white light, pull your second self toward you. Increase the intensity of the light until your second self has fused with you. Turn up the brilliance of the light even more in order to obliterate the scene. Once the scene is gone, note the theme that is meant for your creative meditation. Take three deep breaths, and sigh three times. Record all your experiences and feedback in your journal.

Suggestions for Further Meditations

The guided meditations I have given you here are only a few of the many from which you can choose. Jack Schwarz's book contains a number of wonderful meditations. I suggest you try some. Read them aloud and tape-record them so you can listen to them whenever you wish. At some point you will probably want to create your own guided meditations. Do as your paraconscious mind directs. There is no limit to the meditations you can create specifically for your needs. That means there is no limit to the rewards you can obtain from your meditations. Each meditation not only solves problems and offers guidance; each one opens a new meditation to take you further than you are now. With each meditation, each day becomes an exciting possibility for greater abundance, success, happiness, health and growth.

Meditation is not something done passively. The personal powers and inner resources obtained during applied meditation are the most powerful forces available to you in this universe. When they become a part of you, you can use them every day of your life.

Do not lose faith in the beginning if little or nothing seems to be happening with your meditations. You are changing the way you look at the world. That takes time. On the other hand, when the meditations begin to succeed and work well, do not get intoxicated with them. Meditation is not an escape mechanism; it is a path of action.

You cannot stop with just gaining access to universal intelligence and power. You are more than a mere observer of life. You are creative energy. You are a co-creator. During your voyage on planet earth, you are the creator of your own life and your own self. At your birth your creative source turned your continued creation over to you. You are an important part of a continuous ongoing creation. You are both the creator and the created.

Remember that your purpose in the guided meditation is to use your mind to tap into the limitless reservoir of the universal mind and to find a theme you can use in the most powerful meditation of all, creative meditation. But the guided meditation is a potent tool in and of itself. It can take you to a higher level of mental stimulation and excitement. With it you can feel the touch and breath of your creator at your side. You can be walking and sharing with the greatest force known in this universe, the force that has energized all truly great people and truly great lives.

Living Every Day of Your Life as a Guided Meditation

The guided meditation is a prototype for getting the most out of every day of your life. It is a method whereby we can lift ourselves into a life of higher knowledge and greater abundance.

Every day, from the moment we wake up until the moment we fall asleep, we are guided by our conscious mind. With our concepts and belief systems, all of us are following and living a script—exactly as we did in our guided meditations. However, rarely are we aware of the script we are following. Unfortunately our conscious mind and the ego it has created almost completely blocks out our paraconscious mind function. It is exiled into solitary confinement.

In spite of this, our paraconscious mind always remains in contact with the universal mind. It is ready 24 hours a day to add its wisdom and power to our lives. In the guided meditation we develop our ability to open our self to our paraconscious inflow any time it can be of value to us.

We do this by two methods. First, we can purposely stop our conscious mind input—become an observer—and experience the insight, wisdom and power we then receive from the universal mind. Second, in the guided meditation, without our actively bringing it in, we can open ourselves to allow our paraconscious mind to bring in universal intelligence and change our script whenever "it" wants to.

In each guided meditation we develop our ability to be aware of and use both our conscious and paraconscious mind inputs. In short, we develop our total mind function. When we look at each day of our life as a guided meditation, we can develop our abilities to use the events of our day to continually further develop our total mind function! We will then experience each day as an interplay between our conscious and paraconscious minds. And we experience these interplays as bipolar circuits of creative energy. With each conscious-paraconscious interplay we experience, we also experience the totality of the universe and ourselves.

The guided meditation is a blueprint for how to get the most out of each day by using both our conscious and our paraconscious minds. The guided meditation you did was guided by your conscious mind, just as your everyday life is guided. Yet the paraconscious mind is in contact with the universal mind and is constantly ready to supply you with its wisdom and power. Just as you opened yourself to this power during the guided meditation, you can open yourself to it during your daily life by experiencing each day as a guided meditation.

The point is to become aware that in your daily life you constantly have available to you the power of the paraconscious mind. You undoubtedly have had flashes of intuition or lucky hunches. That is your paraconscious mind, breaking through the noise of your conscious mind. Living each day as a guided meditation you will learn how to listen to your paraconscious mind, not only during meditation, but also in your daily life. The events of your daily life become guided meditations. There is no limit to the opportunities and abundance that will open for you.

Once you become expert at guided meditation, you can live each day of your life as a guided meditation. Each event of your life can become a guided meditation. You will allow your paraconscious mind to continually offer its input. With this ability, any time you feel is proper, you can remove all input from your mind and create a void, a complete silence. Then the paraconscious will bring to you a theme or idea for you to use in a creative meditation which will increase your enlightenment.

Your life becomes a continual interplay between you and the universal mind. It is a continual conversation between you and your creator. This is the deepest bliss you can live! This is the ultimate power available to any human being. It is the ultimate wealth. Achieving this enlightenment and growth, this tremendous personal evolution, is a major purpose of your life on earth.

It is now time for you to do the creative meditation, the final step in your journey into enlightenment and abundance.

8
CREATIVE MEDITATION

Eternity is in love with the productions of time.
—William Blake, "Proverbs of Hell"

Creative meditation is a deep contemplation on the theme you have discovered in your guided meditation. During the creative meditation you will become aware of the wisdom and power in that theme. In it your conscious mind becomes an observer only—a *very* alert and active observer, but it takes no part in directing or guiding the meditation. The only conscious control you exercise is in directing your second self to enter the scene. After the entrance of your second self, the meditation is controlled by the paraconscious mind.

Creative meditation has the potential for bringing the highest and most general intelligence from the universal mind to your self. All of the previous phases of applied active meditation had a purpose in addition to enlightenment. For the creative meditation, enlightenment, in and of itself, is the objective.

The Meaning of Enlightenment
Let me explain what we mean by enlightenment. The material success that we experience is impermanent. It exists only for a short time. As soon as our physical body dies, all our material wealth and power is meaningless. It turns to nothing.

The inescapable recognition of the impermanence of everything in the material world is the greatest cause of human suffering. How can a material life, which is a life of blatant impermanence, be of any value? How can a life of impermanence have any purpose?

The answer, of course, is on the spiritual side of life. Enlightenment is permanent. Enlightenment is the adding to ourself of that which is permanent. Of that which has infinite meaning. Of that which never becomes nothing. Of that which does not leave us when our physical body dies. What are we describing? The addition of universal intelligence and wisdom to our self. That is our eternal abundance.

The Concept of Service to Others

Only through your own enlightenment and empowerment can you be of service to others. For the most part what we call service to others is an ego-created, self-centered, self-rewarding, other-degrading experience. We give the "poor" a meal or a dozen meals. We feel charitable and good about ourselves. But we have not increased our wisdom or power in any way. And we certainly have not increased the wisdom or power of the people we are supposedly helping. This type of service accomplishes three things:

1. It makes the giver feel more powerful and godlike.

2. It increases the dependency of the needy on outside sources. The recipients of this kind of service learn they are so hopeless and powerless that they need outside help for even their basic survival needs.

3. The recipients are degraded. Nothing can lower self-esteem and self-image faster than having to beg for help from other more worthy, more successful people.

There is only one way to be of true service to others and that is through helping and guiding them to self-empowerment. This does not mean we should not help people in need with their basic survival. It means we look at helping them with food and shelter as a means to an end: the end being self-empowerment.

Since nobody can give what he or she does not have, the first step in being of genuine service to others is to empower our self. Then and only then can anyone help others. Only when a person is expert in the process of self-empowerment, can he or she give anything of value to others.

The Permanent Creative Principle

Universal creative intelligence is the permanent substance of the universe. It was not created. It always was, always is and always will be. It is the creator of everything in the universe. It creates everything out of itself. Since each of our physical bodies is unique, each of our physical bodies had to be created from a unique energy source. Since energy cannot be created, this unique energy source had to separate from our universal creative source, which is our universal creative intelligence. Since energy is eternal and cannot be destroyed, the energy source of each of us is eternal. We call your unique creative energy your eternal self. Your eternal self is a unique "package" that separated from the sea of the universal intelligence. That package of universal intelligence created your physical self in order to interact with life on earth and evolve to a higher level of consciousness.

James Clerk Maxwell proved both the existence of electromagnetic waves and that our universe is made-up primarily of these waves. We soon learned that this electromagnetic energy is the creative energy of our universe. Today's laws of physics have shown us that electromagnetic waves carry unlimited information. This information is now called *IS*, which stands for information substance.

However, experiments now being done indicate that electromagnetic waves may not be the basic creative energy source of our universe. They indicate that electromagnetic waves do not carry information, but rather are made-up of information substance. Therefore the basic building block in our universe, and the source of our creative energy, is information! While this research is only beginning, the picture it is presenting validates and fits perfectly into our model.

Through the interactions with our physical self, our eternal self becomes enlightened. Enlightenment is not possible without a physical body and a mind. When our physical body dies, our eternal self is at a higher level of universal intelligence than it was at the birth of the physical body. Then, with the so-called "death" of our physical body, our eternal self can pass on to another adventure somewhere else in the universe to continue its evolution.

We are a manifestation of and an expression of universal intelligence. As Kahlil Gibran wrote: ". . . the human soul is but a part of a burning torch . . . which God separated from Himself at Creation." Our eternal self is a limited amount of universal intelligence. It is only a small package separated from the intelligence that fills the universe. Our purpose, the meaning of our life on earth, is to expand the amount of the universal intelligence that is our eternal self. The process of adding universal intelligence to our permanent self is called enlightenment. It means bringing the light of the universal intelligence into our eternal self. Whatever light we add to our eternal self is permanent. It can never be removed. It never goes away.

Blockages to Enlightenment

The major impediment to enlightenment is ego. Our ego is the image we have of ourself as a complete being separated from, and usually in competition with, all other beings. This ego arises out of the awareness of the transitory nature of our material life. Ego tries to protect you from the knowledge of death. It does everything it can to deny the vulnerability of the physical self.

The ego struggles to maintain a sense of a solid, continuous self. It will interfere with any attempt we make to acknowledge a permanent existence beyond the temporary physical one we now have. If we strive to become spiritual, our ego will try to imitate spirituality and the meditative way of life. This false meditation leads to a false feeling of spirituality and is called spiritual materialism.

It is simple to tell the difference between true meditation and the imitation meditation of the ego. The meditation controlled by the ego aspires primarily to rewards—better health, more wealth, greater happiness, greater spirituality. Imitation meditation does not aim primarily for enlightenment.

Creative Meditation

Creative meditation works on themes and ideas. You present your mind with a theme, and then bring in the universal mind to combine with and react to it. As with the other parts of applied active meditation, you prepare for creative meditation with correct posture and breathing.

When you consciously choose an image, you will find it must first go through a process of transformation before its true nature is revealed. Guided meditation is so important because it accomplishes that transformation. Creative meditation then probes deeper and deeper into the heart of the image and the opportunities it presents.

The earliest part of creative meditation repeats the stages of guided meditation. First, you set up your theme. You are going to use the theme as bait, throwing it into the sea of the universal mind that surrounds you. You can look at your entire earthly life and all its problems primarily as bait for attracting universal intelligence to yourself, and thereby achieving enlightenment.

The Formal Steps

Creative meditation has seven steps, the same seven that you learned for guided meditation: concentration, decentralization, creation of the second self, penetration, contemplation, synthesis and erasure.

Step 1—Concentration

You begin your meditation by creating your horizon and putting your theme on it. A theme can be anything. You are like the beam of light in a slide projector. You project the image or scene outside of yourself and onto a surface that will display all of its details. The stronger your excitement, the farther out you will project your theme.

You are energy. You are concentrating that energy into an image and projecting the image outside yourself. Do not just gaze passively at your horizon. Use the full power of your illumination to propel the image out there. Become excited. Become filled with desire. Become lustful. That's right: lust after what you truly want. The word lust may put you off. But remember, it is an abbreviation of luster. And luster is the glow, the excitement you need to generate energy. So with excitement, with desire, with lust, you project your image onto your horizon. Concentrate on it so you can begin to sense its reality. Visualize every detail: color, form, texture, scent, sound and taste.

By projecting your theme, you have begun to depersonalize it, to become non-attached. You have let it go from your mind, so already you are apart from it. You are an observer, very much interested and concerned, but outside what is happening in front of you.

Step 2—Decentralization

The next step is to decentralize. When you decentralize you remove everything from your mind except the theme. The theme becomes the center of your attention to the exclusion of everything else. It should be as if nothing else in the world exists other than the theme. The image now becomes like circulating energy. It is out there on your horizon, free to move about, to change form, to express the universal mind.

You will notice there is a different meaning to decentralization in creative meditation. In guided meditation, this step was a focusing, a determination not to become distracted by anything that might interfere with the object of concentration. In creative meditation, decentralization is, in addition, the release of the energy within the object of concentration.

As you get into your meditation, almost inevitably, diversionary thoughts will arise in your mind. They will try to distract you from the theme you've projected onto your horizon. You may have been tricked by these thoughts. You may have assumed they would be helpful in solving whatever problem is on your horizon. Generally, though, they are the vestiges of your conscious mind's activity. The conscious mind does not let go easily. It keeps sending signals. Pay no attention. Just let those thoughts pass by. You can recognize them for what they are because they will be the opinions of others. They will be attempting to control you, to make you adhere to the belief systems holding you back.

There are techniques for letting these crippling thoughts go by. You can take a handful of match sticks and throw one match on the ground for every irrelevant thought that enters your mind. Or you can use beads, and toss one out for each thought that distracts you from your purpose. These techniques are ways you can train yourself. Soon you won't need them. You will be able to recognize interference right away and to let it move along without distracting you. You will focus on your projected image to the exclusion of everything else. Focus on your theme and cease to be aware of anything beyond it. You will not question the theme or try to apply logic to what you are seeing. Nor will you evaluate, judge or have any expectations about what is going to happen. Simply concentrate on your topic, and decentralize from any distraction.

Step 3—Creation of your second self

To depersonalize the meditation you will create a second self, an image you will send into the scene to represent you. Take whatever image occurs spontaneously to you. The image may surprise you because it looks totally different from what you expected. It is usually not going to be a mirror image of you. In fact, it may look nothing like your physical self. But it is your second self.

Place that second self between you and your horizon. Now have the second self move onto the horizon and into the scene.

Step 4—Penetration

Your second self entering the scene is called penetration. At first, the second self gets acclimated to the environment you've established. It may not act until you command it to do so. Initially, you are the activator as well as the observer. Once you tell your second self to act, you stop all further conscious mind input and observe throughout the rest of the meditation.

Walking away from you, your second self approaches the image that represents the theme of this meditation. Observe all you can. Momentarily the second self will merge with the image. Watch everything that happens. Note every detail.

As in the guided meditation, remain an objective observer while your second self plays the subjective role in the situation you have created. Do not consciously decide how you should behave. Allow things to happen and observe how your second self handles whatever comes its way. The entire scene is being controlled by paraconscious mind input. Your job is to be the most alert spectator possible.

You will get feedback on various levels as you observe the paraconscious mind at work. You'll notice certain emotions and thoughts. You will also have sensations in various parts of your body. Make note of everything.

After you have been observing intently for awhile, you may not be aware of the difference between you and your second self any longer. Everything the second self does may feel firsthand to you. This means you are in a theta or delta state and receiving an unchecked flow of paraconscious input.

Step 5—Contemplation

Contemplate the scene before you. From outside the action, observe, monitor and record all you see, hear, feel or sense in any way. Do not take any conscious action. Make no evaluation. Cause no alteration in what you observe. Don't try to develop any details by interpreting them. If you do, you will immediately bring in activity from your rational conscious mind, and this inflow will block the universal mind input.

It is also important not to censor or rule out anything you observe. All you perceive is valid. It is essential you learn to acknowledge and validate all the images and information displayed during the meditation. Only then will you hear the voice of the universal mind and know you have escaped the limitations of the conscious mind's rationality.

Contemplation is an intense, non-attached observation. It is a self-regulating process possible only through faith and trust in yourself. You do not need to verify your internal experiences by logical analysis or other people's opinions, because you know that ultimately you are the only truth there is.

You have entered into the field of observation and experience without any conscious effort to make changes. You contemplate the changes taking place in the theme and in the involvement of your second self. Your conscious mind is an excited observer, but takes no part whatsoever in the happenings. The actions and input you are contemplating come from the paraconscious function of your mind.

This contemplation is a very intense observation. I call it passive volition because it is a behavior you bring about with your will. By your will, you stop the input of the conscious function of your mind, while keeping this conscious function as a very active observer of the paraconscious input. This type of passive volition is possible only when you have faith and trust in yourself. Any doubting that arises will result in conscious mind input and end the entire process. You must know that *you* are the ultimate source of your truth.

Step 6—Synthesis

Once the scene is static, and no more changes are coming, the next step is synthesis. You direct pure energy toward the horizon.

After recording all the feedback from the scene, there is within you a joyful excitement from the effect it had on you. You feel that your energy has been activated and has expanded. Now envision and experience your energy radiating into the scene.

Bombard the scene with the purest, highest energy possible. I call this white light energy. Laser beam it. At first your energy surrounds the scene. Then it permeates this spectacle with pure white light. Every detail becomes clearer, and you become more aware of the meaning and purpose of the scene as a whole. All the details are a totality. Your white light is framing and illuminating the scene. You understand what everything has meant. Remember these revelations, but do not pause to consider them. Do not think of yourself as anything but the generator of this strong, pure, white light.

Step 7—Erasure

Keep directing the bright white light as if it were sent from your forehead, like the beam from a miner's helmet—only a hundred fold, a thousand fold, stronger. Let the light become so strong it actually dissolves the scene you have been watching. Your light will shatter all form. Everything will blend into a kind of mist or fog.

Most people have trouble with this step in creative meditation because they feel they are losing what they set up. But lose it you must. To be reborn, you must die. You must destroy the scene you created so the energy is free to come together again in a totally different scene, one that will have new messages for you. You do not want to hang on to past images and events. You want to reintegrate all events into higher powers. So as the scene dissolves and transforms into energy itself, take a last look at it and let it go.

If anything of the scene still remains, consciously erase it. See only white emptiness before you. The moment it all fades and becomes a blank screen, you seemingly have erased it. Yet in reality you actually have transmuted it from its denser state into a bright state of high energy and power. Now your energy becomes totally white, and you immediately get a feeling of well-being. You need go no further.

As the theme is erased you will experience a vision from the universal mind. It is almost a pure inflow of universal mind wisdom, insight and power. It is the deepest and most generalized universal intelligence available to you. It is the most powerful stimulus for personal growth and power accessible on earth!

Your total mind has used your theme as bait for bringing more universal intelligence into your life. You have transmuted yourself to a higher state of energy and power. And you will now respond differently to all situations in your life because you will be operating on that higher level.

To illustrate, we will assume at the conclusion of the guided meditation the vision given you is a burning candle. That means by doing a creative meditation on that vision you will bring to yourself the wisdom, insight and power of virtually pure universal intelligence. So now we will do a candle flame creative meditation.

Candle Flame Meditation

You see a brightness on your horizon. As you expand your gaze you realize it is actually the flame of a candle. Adjust your perspective until you see an entire candle burning in front of you. Contemplate this image and be aware of what it is telling you about your own being.

The oxygen from the air combines with the energy being released from the wick to form a flame. Notice how the wax melts when this happens. The subtle energy and the wax integrate to create visible light.

You are like that candle. You too require the energy from within your body and the oxygen from the atmosphere in order to keep the flame of consciousness burning. All parts of the physical world and all your sensations are indicators of a far more powerful existence, too subtle to be experienced in itself. The oxygen you breathe, for example, is symbolic of the universal creative intelligence. Thus every breath you draw into your body is a symbolic expression of drawing the vital energy of universal creative intelligence into your being.

When you focus on your breathing, you become aware of subtle transformations within you. Then you experience the merging of the external and internal energies in your spine (like the candlewick), and the resulting expansion of energy fills your head with light (like the candle flame). The higher the flame—the more energy (drawn from both sources and harmoniously integrated)—the brighter your awareness will be. Just as the candle illumines the darkness, you radiate the degree of enlightenment you have attained. So to intensify energy means literally to expand consciousness, thereby lighting your way and that of fellow travelers.

From this meditation I was told my missions in life are first to continually empower myself, and second to radiate the universal intelligence that empowered me so others can benefit. This book is a part of that mission. This is the type of wisdom and power, of enlightenment, one can achieve from a creative meditation.

This point is wonderfully illustrated in a story from another book I highly recommend, *Jacob the Baker,* by Noah benShea:

> *A neighbor of Jacob's needed to start on a journey, but it was the middle of the night.*
>
> *Afraid to begin, afraid not to begin, he went to Jacob.*
>
> *"There is no light on the path," he complained.*
>
> *"Take someone with you," counseled Jacob.*
>
> *"Jacob, what do you mean? If I do that, there will be two blind men."*
>
> *"You are wrong," said Jacob. "If two people discover each other's blindness, it is already growing light."*

A Journey of Becoming

Review is an important final stage in creative meditation. Remember what happened and try to understand and integrate it. Integrating it can take some time because doing so requires action. Creative meditation is complete only when you experience it by acting upon the insights you have gained from the universal mind. Each time you get new feedback from the world, which is a continuous process, you review and integrate it. So creative meditation is a spiral that begins when you take conscious responsibility for your life and set your whole aim on self-knowledge and the evolution of your eternal self.

With time and practice, guided and creative meditations will become a routine part of your daily life! Total integration of meditation into your everyday life is the purpose of this entire process. As you continue to meditate, visions and themes should come to you ten, twenty, fifty times a day. Almost any thought, any vision, any idea you experience can be the basis for a creative meditation.

Ultimately meditations will guide your every action. They will have continuity and integrity. They will be a seamless part of your life, not limited to certain times of day or certain subjects. It will be as if your daily life is the horizon of your meditation. All day long you are observing it, experiencing it, using it as a stepping stone to a higher level. Without ever stopping, you will have creative inspiration and universal power and intelligence flowing through you.

When creative meditation becomes the way you live your life, you will know total abundance, true bliss, life at its fullest. Remember, you are the universe. Therefore you are meant to be a perfect conducting instrument—a channel of energy free of obstruction—between yourself and the universal mind. You are limited in this by only one factor—the level of your consciousness. When you know and accept this, you will use applied active meditation to daily and continually interact with universal intelligence. By so doing you will grow materially by raising your level of consciousness and personal power. And at the same time you will grow spiritually by raising the level of consciousness and enlightenment of your eternal self.

The more you grow spiritually, the more the forces and amazing powers of the universal mind are yours to use. The more you live, the more you become one with your universe, one with "god," and the more your life is a journey of becoming. When you live your meditations, the very powers that control the universe are at your disposal!

9
STEPS TOWARD A CO-CREATIVE LIFE

> *Man was made for Joy and Woe;*
> *And when this we rightly know,*
> *Thro' the World we safely go,*
> *Joy and woe are woven fine,*
> *A clothing for the soul divine.*
> —William Blake, "Auguries of Innocence"

Somewhere during the different phases of meditation you've been learning in this workbook, you will discover what life is. You will know the secret of living a completely fulfilling and successful life. You will realize life has not one, but two aspects to it. You have been aware of the material aspect of your life. Now you are getting in touch with the non-material, spiritual aspect of your life. To live life to its fullest means living in *both* aspects. You will know you can call on an amazing life force, a power great enough to propel you to your highest level of consciousness. The amazing life force you encounter will apply to both the material and non-material aspects of your life. On the material side, it will bring health, happiness, wealth, excitement and success. On the non-material side, the reward is ever-increasing enlightenment, which leads to a life of joy and ecstasy.

Understanding and Growing
Toward Illumination

If you have been practicing any of the facets of applied active meditation, you are undoubtedly experiencing greater personal power, increased harmony and spiritual evolution and growth.

132

I have talked about the circuit of self-empowerment, whereby universal intelligence is transmuted into personal power. Another way of thinking about this cycle is to use the three I's: intuition, insight and inspiration.

Intuition is the tuning in by your paraconscious mind to universal intelligence. *Insight* is the transfer of paraconscious mind input to the subconscious mind. *Inspiration* is the powerful plan of action that rounds out the process. The word "inspire" literally means to set on fire. In the dictionary, *inspiration* is defined as "the divine influence on a person." When, by the use of universal intelligence, you glow and shine—you are indeed inspired.

The Act of Co-creation

With the use of applied active meditation, you are awakening to your co-creatorship with the universal mind. Once you realize you are the source of more creation, you cannot deny the existence within yourself of the force that created you. You are then one with that force. Applied active meditation leads you directly into this oneness with your creator.

With each creative act, you increase your ability to create. This assures a constant inflow of power from your paraconscious mind and the universal mind. Thus there is never a separation between you and your creator. By your creative acts, you add power and strength both to yourself and to the universe. Instead of looking only to the outer world for signs of your power, you become aware of your inner creative world, of your immense inner powers.

By using applied active meditation you increase your ability to use the total mind, and by so doing, your own inner creative powers increase. Your goal is to obtain from the universal mind those particular powers and insights you require to fulfill your purpose as co-creator. Remember, universal creative intelligence is not something "out there," separate from you. The universal mind is *you*. You are made-up of the same creative force that makes up the universe. You are the same creative force as your creator, which means that— while at a different level—you are also a creative force and a creator. Your level of consciousness is admittedly small, though, compared with universal creative intelligence.

You are here to expand that level by co-creative acts. You have a responsibility to nurture and actualize every creative seed within you. Every creative act carries with it the seed of the next creative act. If you stop acting and just start living on the success of one creative act, you will stop growing.

Each of us has a path of action to follow. Your path is just as individual as you are. It consists of all your co-creative acts. Your path of co-creative action is a path of personal development and expansion, as well as evolution of your eternal self.

Using the processes you are now learning and doing, you can combine almost every event in your life with these great universal powers, and by so doing turn your life into a creative journey leading to abundance.

How the Pieces of Applied Active Meditation Work Together

Applied active meditation consists of separate processes. You will know which process best fits your particular needs after becoming familiar with all of them. The cosmic review and the psycho-physical rehearsal will remain useful to you even after you have arrived at the plateau of creative meditation.

The cosmic review empties your mind of the garbage and negative events that have collected the past day, so when you do the creative meditation, or any other meditation, you are able to gain access to more universal intelligence and power. The cosmic review informs your subconscious mind of what the universal mind would have done in situations that caused you concern from the previous day. The cosmic review connects the universal mind to your everyday life. It connects your daily negative events with their positive events in the universal mind, and your positive events with higher enlightenment. This review unleashes your potential to be an energy-conducting instrument in contact with the entire universe. Every force is both positive and negative. When the positive and negative are connected and turned on by action, they yield an enormous flow of creative energy and power.

The psycho-physical rehearsal has a piece for the present and one for the future. There is also the autogenic psycho-physical rehearsal. The present time psycho-physical rehearsal brings the universal mind into what you are doing right now, at this moment. Whether you are speaking to another person, attending a meeting or giving a lecture, with the psycho-physical rehearsal you can use the paraconscious function of your mind to add intelligence from the universal mind to your subconscious mind to affect what is now taking place in your life.

Since the cosmic review can be done in isolation with no distractions, it is easier to learn than the active psycho-physical rehearsal. That is why I suggest you first become proficient in cosmic review. Then, when you feel you are ready, try applying the psycho-physical rehearsal to a present moment in your life. The present moment psycho-physical rehearsal is a major source of increased intelligence from the universal mind. Using it, you will discover you can tune into the universal mind at any time and for any event you desire and express it immediately.

When you apply the psycho-physical rehearsal to your future, you add intelligence from the universal mind to your mind. The autogenic psycho-physical rehearsal takes you beyond the focus of the other two rehearsals. It allows you to gather intelligence from the universal mind for use whenever you need it, and to make this gathering a regular part of your daily routine.

Four Basic Techniques for Meditation

Here are four basic techniques you must become familiar with to get the most out of your meditations:

1. Projecting a horizon and creating a scene
2. Relaxing—assuming the proper posture so physical sensations do not interfere with your concentration
3. Breathing for an aware, contemplative state
4. Reviewing—analyzing the meditative experience so *it can be validated and applied to daily life*

Projecting Your Horizon

In the cosmic review, you learned how to project your horizon and set up some kind of screen for rolling a film of your day's events. In all the other parts of applied active meditation, you will do something similar. You may not always have a screen, but the action you see will appear outside of you and will be like watching a movie. You must feel as if you are the projector and the audience. You are objective about what is occurring on your horizon.

When you observe an event and feel it to be a negative occurrence, stop the film. Look at this frozen moment in time. Study the single image. Stop any input from your conscious mind and meditatively open your paraconscious mind to the universal mind. Allow the universal mind to bring into your mind the positive side of the negative occurrence. See the solution as it occurs before you.

Perceive the wholeness of the situation. This means moving beyond your initial judgment of the situation as negative. Experience this negative situation as an opportunity, as a source through which you can now receive greater universal power.

During this experience, become aware of any energy-blocking feelings, such as guilt, fear, low self-esteem, doubts. Weed these out by becoming non-attached to them. By objectively observing them with no emotional input from your conscious mind, you can let them go.

Now become aware of the incoming universal intelligence and resonate in harmony with the positive intelligence and power being brought to you. In front of you, on your screen, observe yourself taking the actions dictated by the universal mind. Watch the results.

If the results are not totally appropriate, repeat the exercise. Even if you think they are appropriate, you might still want to repeat the exercise because usually on the repeats you will discover negative emotions that were hidden the first time. Acknowledge what you have learned from the situation. Be aware of your reaction to it. Then roll the movie again. You will experience it differently. You will experience things you missed the first time through.

Relaxing

Sit, stand and walk erect. Straighten your spine. Hold your head erect on your spine with your shoulders back. No slouching forward. This is necessary to free your diaphragm so you can breathe from it.

The goals of correct posture are to allow for the free flow of energy and breath, to disperse tension and to conserve energy. Pockets of tension in your body interfere with the flow of energy. They also can create in your mind a conscious awareness of your body.

The relationship of relaxation to awareness is important. The achievement of relaxation is a major objective of meditation. Without it, any success you have with meditation—or in any area of your life—will be limited. Relaxation can open new dimensions of health and success for you.

Illness is a loss of life energy to the affected cells. When the energy is lost, the cells forget how to function. Awareness of correct function comes to the cells from the free flow of life energy, which carries enormous amounts of information. If this information does not get through because of an energy blockage, the cells lose their way.

Whenever you feel threatened, irritated or opposed by the outside world, your body responds with a contraction reaction. The entire body, down to each individual cell, contracts. The great physiologist Walter Cannon called this the "fight or flight" reaction. Wilhelm Reich called it "body armor."

This contraction serves to define the boundary between you and the rest of the world and to maintain you as a separate entity. It creates a barrier between you and the things and people you come in contact with. According to your ego, you "need" this barrier to protect yourself from a hostile world.

However, it impedes the flow of life energy through the body. The absence of contraction allows for the free flow of life energy. The life energy then brings to each cell the awareness of how to function correctly and—since each cell dies—creates an organizing field that will replace dead cells with properly working ones.

Contraction lowers your resistance. For example, you touch a hot stove and your muscles contract. You have a burn. With contracted muscles, you offered no resistance to the excess heat and its ability to burn. If, however, you were relaxed, the heat would do little if any damage. By not going into a contraction reaction, you could increase the flow of life energy to the area, which would increase your resistance to the heat. With that powerful energy field around you, there would be little harm the heat could do to you.

When I talk about relaxation, I mean relaxation with energy flow. This is more than mere muscle relaxation. By itself, muscle relaxation does not increase the energy. Instead it results in a kind of flaccid immobility. The kind of relaxation I'm talking about keeps the body functional and increases the energy flow. Your muscles are relaxed, but you can also feel the energy moving through you. Total relaxation does not mean going limp. It means responding and acting strongly, but with the entire body in a relaxed state.

When you are relaxed and your energy flow is high, you do not experience barriers between you and the outside world. Rather, you feel a continual flow between you and the outside world. You feel as one.

A major achievement of meditation in any of its forms, be it cosmic review, psycho-physical rehearsal, guided or creative meditation, is to achieve total relaxation with increased life energy flow. This is a major source of strength. In your meditations, please become aware of this feeling. When you do, you will experience the great increase in power and successes that comes with total relaxation. You will live a life of abundance and bliss.

Breathing

Proper breathing helps to bring in more intelligence from the universal mind. The longer the length of the brain wave you radiate, the more intelligence from the universal mind it will bring back when it returns to you. Thus to effectively bring in intelligence from the universal mind, you must be at least in an alpha state. Theta will bring in more than alpha, and delta more than both.

Most important is high voltage power or amplitude. With low voltage, radiation at any level will bring back little, if any, intelligence from the universal mind. The higher the voltage, the more powerful will be the intelligence from the universal mind that resonates with you. Since high voltage is the direct result of excitement, faith, commitment and discipline—you must practice all of these to their fullest.

The greater the intelligence from the universal mind brought to you, the higher your level of consciousness will be. Thus the higher the amplitude of your radiation and the deeper toward delta brain waves you get, the higher the level of consciousness and intelligence available to you will be. So keep developing your breathing toward higher amplitude and longer brain wave frequencies.

Once you have achieved a breathing pattern you are comfortable and happy with and your body can exercise it comfortably, cease concentrating on it. When you get your breathing pattern regulated, give your full attention to the meditation.

Reviewing

Whenever feasible, after any meditative exercise or experience, analyze and review it. I recommend this series of questions:

Mental observations: What were the mental obstacles? What thoughts arose to interrupt my concentration?

Physical feedback: What were the physical obstacles? Did I become aware of any pressure, pain or tingling sensation at any time? Why did this particular sensation accompany that particular aspect of the experience?

Emotional response: Did I become emotionally involved with any aspect of the experience? Did this emotion arise at the same time as, before or after any physical sensation? Why did the feeling occur in the context of that physical sensation?

By writing down and dating these experiences, you will have a record of each phase of your development. You will be aware of change. Some negative responses, such as stomach aches, may disappear. Others, such as crying, may increase. You may wish to illustrate your journal with drawings or colors of your meditative experiences.

Key Concept: Transcendence

Transcendence is the way to enlightenment. Do not expect this way to be painless. Understanding the nature of suffering is one of the first insights you must have in order to evolve. Many philosophies have taught that enlightenment comes only through suffering.

This does not mean, however, that you should create suffering for yourself. As soon as you do, you resonate on the same low level as the suffering you create, plus you bring more and more suffering into your life.

The suffering that will come inevitably into your life can increase your awareness of a greater order of events than those that caused your pain to begin with. Through this awareness, you can achieve a higher state. You can increase your insights. When you acquire such understanding, you can break your attachment to the emotions that have clogged your energy flow and lowered your resonance. The clogged energy flow and lowered resonance keep you functioning in a lower field, one of suffering and failure.

Every experience you have ever had is stored away in your subconscious mind, along with its accompanying feelings. You can never get rid of an experience, and you can never change it. Every experience you have affects you for the rest of your life. The pain and sorrow associated with negative experiences can block the flow of creative energy if you don't make an effort to transcend those experiences. Transcending hurtful experiences is not getting rid of them. It is converting their negative effect to a positive, to an increase in energy flow.

One big question for most of you has been, *Where do I find positive experiences to join to the negatives that are plaguing my life?* By now, you should be aware of the enormous resource available to you in the sea of the universal mind which surrounds and moves through you. Using your paraconscious mind, you tune into the universal mind. The negative experience is stored in your subconscious. Your paraconscious finds its positive counterpart in the universal mind.

The paraconscious then transfers the positive into your subconscious. There it connects with the negative experience. As a result of the connection, you will feel a surge of power. To make the positive yours you must experience it. You experience it by taking the action designed by the universal mind. The action is the light switch that turns on the current and gets it flowing.

Transcending Positive Events

Achieving enlightenment is not limited to transcending negative events. Any strong desire or need you have can be a source for enlightenment. The process is the same. Place your desire into your conscious-subconscious mind. Then let your paraconscious mind bring in the universal intelligence that relates to your desire. The universal mind will have a positive expression of your desire. When that positive expression is joined with the outline of your desire, you can then act according to the guidance offered by the universal mind. You will achieve your dream and desire and have more power and insight available to you for other dreams and desires.

In the same way, positive experiences can lead to enlightenment. In fact, enlightenment from positive events and actions is a basic step on the path of action. To gain enlightenment from positive experiences, you must continually transcend your successes. If you are satisfied with having reached one goal and you stop there, your journey of enlightenment will be at an end.

To continue your journey means you never reach a state of happiness in which you wish to remain, to which you become attached. You *renounce and enjoy*. Whenever you achieve your positive result, no matter how wonderful, you tune into your paraconscious mind and the universal mind to see how you can use that action or event as a base for achieving even greater happiness and success. There is no end to your journey of enlightenment nor to your possible abundance.

Every time you practice transcendence, you become a more powerful and more aware human being. Thus with every transcension, you die. You will not emerge from the experience the same person you were before. You will die and be reborn as a more powerful, more aware human being.

Bringing "God" into View

Through creative meditation, you can directly experience the universal intelligence that created the universe and everything in it. In the Judeo-Christian tradition, this universal mind is known as God. The obvious difference between you and God is that God operates at a much, much higher level of consciousness, and therefore has immensely greater power and intelligence. But your presence on earth in a physical body is your opportunity to tap into the greater awareness and power God has and add it to your own awareness and power, thus becoming more like God, more one with your creator.

You are not only a creation of an all-knowing universal mind, but also an expression of it. Your level of personal creative energy, which is your eternal self, is an expression of universal creative energy. Your purpose on earth is to grow in the power of your expression. Your purpose is to bring God into view. When you use your life to express the creative power that is God, you will be on a path of action that leads to ever greater heights. As soon as you achieve a higher level, you will be moving upward toward the next peak. Each step on the path of action brings greater abundance and prepares you to take the next step.

10

THE APPLIED
ACTIVE MEDITATION PARADIGM

He who binds to himself a Joy
Doth the winged life destroy,
But he who kisses the Joy as it flies
Lives in Eternity's sunrise.

—William Blake, "MS. Notebooks"

A paradigm is a model or pattern a person follows. The paradigm I am about to discuss is a model of how the universe works, and how human beings can most happily and successfully live in it. This model explains that individual lives have a purpose that can be known and achieved.

Obviously, in today's world, there are many different paradigms about how the universe works and what place humans have in it. The paradigm you will now see is a composite of the experiences of many people who have made circuits of self-empowerment a part of their lives.

A hypothesis about the meaning of life and how to live it to its fullest is not one that can be measured by instruments in a scientific laboratory. It can, however, be tested and evaluated. First, you must build a model, then put it into action. You will have associated specific desirable outcomes with the functional model, which is then subject to three tests. If the model passes those tests, you know it is valid. If it fails, then the model is not one you can successfully use at this time.

The first test: is the outcome from using the model your desired outcome? Is it superior to your desired outcome? If so, continue using it. If not, stop the testing right here. This model is not going to work for you.

The second test: when you use the model, does it increase your desire and your excitement? If use of the model makes you feel more alive and spontaneous, continue with it. If it doesn't, stop. You will not reach the state of non-attachment necessary for the model to succeed. Unless this model results in strong desires and high excitement, it is not the model for you.

The third and most important test: Does the model produce predictable results? Can you predict the achievement of a desired outcome? When the model becomes predictable, you can accept it as totally valid for you. It has proven itself.

The applied active meditation paradigm presented in this book has consistently passed all three tests. Since this paradigm has worked so well for so many of us, we are naturally eager to pass it along to you. In summary form, then, here is the paradigm on which this process has been built.

The Paradigm

1. Since every human being is unique, each of us must have been created from a unique source.

2. The primary, undiluted, pure substance out of which the entire universe is composed is electromagnetic energy, expressed in the form of electromagnetic waves. This is a scientific fact.

3. The empty space of the universe has been shown by Maxwell to be packed full of electromagnetic energy in the form of electromagnetic waves.

4. The two basic functional laws of the universe are continual change and harmony. Therefore, although the universe is constructed of a pure energy, to obey universal law, that energy is undergoing constant change.

5. If constant change did not occur, the universe would become one pure, undifferentiated mass of amorphous energy, and it would cease to exist. For energy to have power and to exist, it must be in a state of constant change.

6. The changes that occur result in processes of differentiation. Packages of universal energy separate from the total universal electromagnetic energy field. Each package of energy that

separates from the basic universal electromagnetic field is unique and different from every other package.

7. Each individual package of electromagnetic energy must now also follow the universal laws of change and harmony.

8. Each universal electromagnetic wave carries in it universal intelligence and universal power. There are two types of power: creative power and kinetic or physical power.

9. The longer each wave of universal electromagnetic energy, the more intelligence and creative power it carries. The shorter the wave, the greater its kinetic or physical power.

10. To obey universal law, each individualized package of energy must continually change. But there is a very important corollary to that law: the change must be in the direction of evolution.

11. To evolve means to reach a higher state by becoming more. How does an individual package of universal energy become more? It becomes more by adding to itself universal intelligence and creative power from the surrounding universal electromagnetic field.

12. Every time universal energy is added to the individualized package of energy, it becomes more like the universal energy field from which it originally separated. In all religions this basic energy field is given a name. Western religions call it God. Each time universal energy is added to an individualized package of energy, the individualized package becomes more Godlike.

13. Every human being is unique because every human is created by and from an individualized energy package. This package of universal energy is your non-material self. It builds and creates each of your material selves.

14. This unique energy package that created you also has many names. The most popular is soul or spirit. I particularly like the name of *thou self*, which was given to it by Martin Buber.

15. The soul builds each of your material selves for a specific reason. Your soul or thou self created your physical body as a vehicle by which your soul can evolve. To evolve is to increase the universal intelligence and creative power in your soul. The soul requires a physical body in order to change and evolve.

16. Once your soul acquires additional universal energy and creative power, that addition is permanent. The energy growth of your soul is permanent because your soul is permanent. Being pure

energy, your soul can never be destroyed or die. It can only be transformed. And by universal law the only direction of this transformation is toward higher evolution.

17. Thus in each day of your life, your soul can do either of two things: it can add intelligence from the universal mind and evolve, or it can remain where it is.

18. In order to evolve, the soul must use the physical body, which is material and as such exists only for a limited time. The power you add to your physical body is temporary because your physical body is temporary. The universal power you add to your soul is permanent, because your energy self is your permanent self.

19. Since you are in reality your permanent self, which is your thou self, and your physical self is a vehicle you temporarily use for a specific purpose, what happens when the physical body ceases to exist? As long as the physical body exists, the soul is tied to it. Once the physical body ceases to exist, the soul is free to move on to its next level. At that next level your soul, which is your real and permanent self, will create another vehicle to continue your growth. What that vehicle will be, or where in the universe it will be, depends on the universal energy level the soul has attained when the body dies. With the limited knowledge available to us during our voyage on earth, we have no way of even guessing where your soul, which we call your eternal self, can go or what it will do next to continue your evolution. However, one thing you can be sure of is that you'll find out soon enough.

20. The process by which your soul evolves is specific. The body it created is in contact with the physical world. The mind it created is in contact with the sea of the universal mind. Evolution requires an interaction between these two realms. The interaction between the physical world and the universal mind works like this:

   a. The paraconscious mind gains access to the universal mind, resonates in harmony with it and brings its intelligence back to your subconscious.

   b. The subconscious mind becomes aware of the universal intelligence brought to it. If at this stage your conscious mind becomes active and questions or alters the universal intelligence brought to your subconscious, the process immediately ceases, and that universal energy is no longer available for your use.

c. When the pure intelligence from the universal mind brought to the subconscious is not questioned or altered, it enters the subconscious and is filed there, shuffled in with all past and present intelligence.

d. The subconscious mind uses this added intelligence to devise new and more powerful plans, which it sends to the conscious mind.

e. To complete the process, the conscious mind must act upon the new plan spontaneously. As before, if the conscious mind doubts or alters this plan of action, the cycle is broken and the universal energy is no longer available for your use.

f. When the conscious mind spontaneously acts on the new plan of action, intelligence from the universal mind is transformed into personal intelligence and becomes part of your physical body for as long as it exists. At the same time, the universal energy is radiated into your soul and becomes a permanent part of it. This is how the soul evolves.

g. There is no such thing as a final successful evolution. Each time you have completed a cycle, you become more powerful and the energy you radiate is more powerful. So the universal energy it vibrates with and brings back to you is also more powerful. Each new cycle increases your power and moves you to a higher level, from which you will begin the next cycle.

21. Your mind is much larger than your body. It surrounds your body and extends well beyond it. Your mind also is in every cell in your body. It flows through your entire body. Therefore, all of your body is in your mind, but not all of your mind is in your body!

22. Your mind is the intermediary between your brain and the universal mind.

23. With the techniques of applied active meditation, you create an environment in which your conscious mind can learn to act spontaneously upon the universal intelligence brought to it by the paraconscious mind.

24. The major achievement in life is the addition of intelligence from the universal mind to your permanent self, your soul. Any

success you achieve in your material life—if that success came in accordance with the universal laws of change and harmony—becomes a part of your permanent self. Long after your material body has finished the job for which it was created, the universal intelligence and creative power it attracted remain a part of your permanent self.

These twenty-four points make up the applied active meditation paradigm. When you choose to adopt the paradigm and take the applied active meditation path, you become more one with other human beings, with the universe and with the creative energy that made you. Your soul and spirit bloom. You achieve material success, but you do so in unity and harmony, sharing with others rather than competing.

My hope is this book will serve as a map for you at the beginning of your journey. It is a map I have made from my own explorations. I offer it to you as one way into a vast unexplored territory. If you decide to take the journey for yourself, you will create your own map as you go. It is a sacred journey and one that has as many dimensions as the souls who undertake it.

You will know your way by your progress. As you experience oneness and eternity, as you find your stress and sickness disappearing, you will know you have found the route for you. Proceed with excitement and joy. Your life will never be the same again! It will be abundantly better!

SUGGESTED READING

Barash, David P. *The Hare and the Tortoise*. New York: Viking, 1986.

benShea, Noah. *Jacob the Baker*. New York: Ballantine Books, 1989.

benShea, Noah. *Jacob's Journey*. New York: Villard Books, 1991.

Blake, William. *The Complete Poetry and Prose of William Blake*. Edited by David V. Erdman. Berkeley: University of California Press, 1982.

Buber, Martin. *I and Thou*. New York: Macmillan, 1987.

Burr, Harold Saxton. *Blueprint for Immortality*. London: Neville Spearman, 1972.

Chopra, Deepak. *Quantum Healing*. New York: Bantam Books, 1989.

Dass, Ram. *Journey of Awakening*. New York: Bantam Books, 1990.

Dyer, Wayne. *Real Magic*. New York: Harper Collins, 1992.

Dyer, Wayne. *You'll See It When You Believe It*. New York: William Morrow, 1989.

Dyer, Wayne. *The Sky's the Limit*. New York: Simon and Schuster, 1980.

Emerson, Ralph Waldo. *Essay on Self-Reliance*. In many books with Emerson's essays.

Frankl, Viktor E. *Man's Search for Meaning*. New York: Pocket Books, 1984.

Frankl, Viktor E. *The Unheard Cry for Meaning*. New York: Pocket Books, 1978.

Frankl, Viktor E. *The Will to Meaning*. New York: Meridian, 1988.

Grant, Dave. *The Ultimate Power*. Old Tappan, N.J.: Fleming H. Revell, 1983.

Grant, Dave. *The Great Lover's Manifesto*. Eugene, Oregon: Harvest House, 1986.

Green, Elmer and Alyce. *Beyond Biofeedback*. New York: Dell Publishing, 1977.

Green, Elmer and Alyce. "The Ins and Outs of Mind-Body Energy." *Science Year: The World Book Science Annual*. Chicago: Field Enterprises, 1974.

Hazen, Robert M. and Trefil, James. *Science Matters*. New York: Doubleday, 1991.

Hill, Napoleon. *Think and Grow Rich*. New York: Hawthorn Books, 1972.

Hill, Napoleon. *You Can Work Your Own Miracles*. New York: Fawcett, 1971.

Jaffe, Dennis. *Healing from Within*. New York: Simon and Schuster, 1980.

Johnson, Crocket. *Barnaby. Vols 1-6*. New York: Ballantine, 1985-86.

Justice, Blair. *Who Gets Sick?* Los Angeles: Jeremy Tarcher, 1988.

Kaplan, Aryeh. *Jewish Meditation. A Practical Guide*. New York: Schocken Books, 1985.

Kaplan, Aryeh. *Meditation and Kabbalah*. York Beach, Maine: Samuel Weiser, 1985.

Kohn, Alfie. *No Contest: The Case Against Competition*. Boston: Houghton Mifflin, 1986.

Langer, Ellen J. *Mindfulness*. New York: Addison Wesley, 1990.

LeShan, Lawrence. *How to Meditate*. New York: Bantam Books, 1975.

LeShan, Lawrence. *Alternate Realities*. New York: Ballantine, 1988.

Lewis, C.S. *The Screwtape Letters*. New York: Macmillan, 1982.

Luthe, W. and Schultz, J.H. *Autogenic Therapy. Volume II: Medical Applications*. New York: Grune & Stratton, 1969.

Nesfield-Crookson, Bernard. *William Blake: Prophet of Universal Brotherhood*. Great Britain: Crucible, 1987.

Pert, Candace B. "The Wisdom of the Receptors: Neuropeptides, the Emotions, and Bodymind." *Advances*. Institute for the Advancement of Health. Summer, 1986.

Popp, Fritz-Albert. *Electromagnetic Bio-Information*. Munchen and Baltimore: Urban & Schwarenberg, 1979.

Popp, Fritz-Albert. Personal communication. Munich, Germany: April 22, 1985.

Ringer, Robert J. *Million Dollar Habits*. New York: Fawcett Crest, 1990.

Robbins, Anthony. *Unlimited Power*. New York: Fawcett, 1986.

Satir, Virginia. *Peoplemaking*. Palo Alto, California: Science and Behavior Books, 1972.

Satir, Virginia. *The New Peoplemaking*. Mountain View, California. Science and Behavior Books, 1988.

Schwarz, Jack. *It's Not What You Eat, but What Eats You*. Berkeley: Celestial Arts, 1988.

Schwarz, Jack. *The Path of Action*. New York: E.P. Dutton, 1977.

Schwarz, Jack. *Voluntary Controls*. New York: E.P. Dutton, 1978.

Schwarz, Jack. *Human Energy Systems*. New York: E.P. Dutton, 1980.

Schwarz, Jack. *The Power of Personal Health*. New York: Penguin, 1992.

Schwarz, Jack. *I Know From My Heart*. Berkeley: Celestial Arts, 1992.

Steiner, Rudolf. *Knowledge of the Higher Worlds and Its Attainment*. Hudson, N.Y.: Anthroposophic Press, 1947.

Steiner, Rudolf. *The Stages of Higher Knowledge*. Spring Valley, N.Y.: Anthroposophic Press, 1967.

Strauch, Ralph. *The Reality Illusion*. Barrytown, New York: Station Hill Press, 1989.

Trefil, James. *Reading the Mind of God*. New York: Scribners, 1989.

Trungpa, Chogyam. *Cutting Through Spiritual Materialism*. Boulder, Colorado: Shambala, 1973.

INDEX

A

AAM (*See* Applied Active
　Meditation)
Abundance 1-3, 6, 9-10, 20,
　46-47, 63, 71, 79, 118-
　20, 122, 130, 134, 137,
　140
Adrenal gland 32, 69
Aging 65-66
Alpha brain wave states 16,
　18, 33-34, 36-38, 40,
　108, 137
Alpha breathing 37-38
"A Memorable Fantasy" 44
"A Poison Tree" 22
Applied Active Meditation
　(AAM) 1-2, 6, 9-10, 19,
　22-23, 25, 27, 30, 40,
　44-45, 57, 59, 69, 80,
　83, 90, 95, 100-01, 121,
　131, 133-35, 141-42,
　145-46
　log sheet for 24
Applied Active Meditation
　Paradigm 141-46
Appropriate forces (*See also*
　Inappropriate forces)
　25, 27, 29

"Auguries of Innocence" 31,
　80, 132
Autogenic Psycho-physical
　rehearsal 45, 80-97,
　134-35
　exercises 84-94
　swimming 90-93
　talk show 93-94
　walking #1 85-87
　walking #2 87-88
　walking #3 88-90
　healing 95

B

Belief systems 13-14, 19, 23,
　47, 49-51, 55, 64, 68,
　78, 87, 99, 118, 126
benShea, Noah 130
Beta brain wave states 16,
　18, 32, 36-37
Beta breathing 37
Blake, William 1, 22, 31, 44,
　57, 80-82, 98, 121, 132,
　141, 153-54
Blueprint for Immortality 4
"Book of Thel, The" 98
Brain wave
　amplitude 16
　frequency 16

Breathing 20, 31-41, 49, 95, 102-03, 109, 124, 129, 135, 137-38
  Alpha-Theta transfer 38
  exercises 36-41
  rhythms 35-41
  six levels of
    complete breath 32-35
    correct breathing 32, 35
    full breathing 34, 36-37
    high breathing 31-32
    low-breathing 32-33, 36-37
    mid-breathing 31-33
Buber, Martin 143
Buddhist law of Maya 15
Burr, Dr. Harold Saxton 4, 7

C

Campbell, Joseph 2
Candle flame meditation 129-30
Cannon, Walter 136
Clavicular breathing (*See* Breathing, Six levels of, high breathing)
Circuit of self-empowerment 17-19, 26, 29-30, 46, 48, 56, 59, 80-81, 94, 133
Co-creation 11, 132-34
Conscious mind 11-18, 25-27, 29, 35, 37, 45-47, 49, 51, 53-56, 59, 61-63, 65-68, 70-71, 74, 79, 81-85, 87-88, 90-91, 93-94, 99-106, 109, 111, 116, 118-19, 121, 125-27, 135-36, 139, 144-45
Cosmic review 20, 24, 40, 44-56, 61-62, 76-78, 80, 83, 95-96, 98, 100, 134-35

creating your horizon 49-50
examples 52-54
Letting the Day's Events Roll 50-52
summary 55-56
Creative Energy 4-8, 10, 19, 28, 114, 118-19, 123, 139-40, 146
Creative Meditation 45, 96-100, 121-31
  formal steps 124-31
    candle flame meditation 129-30
    concentration 125
    contemplation 127
    creation of second self 126
    decentralization 125-26
    erasure 128-29
    penetration 126-27
    review 130-31
    synthesis 128

D

Dass, Ram 81
Delta brain wave states 16-18, 36, 39-41, 49, 58, 102-03, 106, 108, 114-16, 127, 137-38
Delta breathing 39
Diaphragm 33-35, 38-39, 90, 136
Diaphragmatic breathing (*See* Breathing, six levels of, low-breathing)
DNA 4-5
Dyer, Wayne 81

E

Edison, Thomas 17
Ego 11, 13, 38, 93, 118, 122, 124, 136

Electromagnetic radiation 3-7, 57-58, 123, 142-43, 154
Endocrine system 32
Enlightenment 45, 97, 99, 102, 120-24, 129-32, 134, 138-40
Entropy 8
Eternal self 7-13, 19, 29, 38, 43, 66, 93, 123, 130-31, 134, 140, 144
"Everlasting Gospel, The" 1
Evolution 8-9, 11, 19, 23, 43, 66, 72, 83-84, 95, 108, 120, 123, 130, 132, 134, 143-45
Excitement factor 17-18, 41-42

F

Frankl, Viktor 81

G

Gibran, Kahlil 54, 123
God 6, 11-12, 123, 131, 140, 143, 155
Gonadal system 32
Guided meditation 21, 45, 96, 98-121, 124-26
   clay statue 106-08
   cube and sphere 115
   formal steps 104-05
   mountain exercise 108-14
   process 101-04
   river and cavern exercise 114
   seven door exercise 116-17

H

Harmony 9, 46-47, 55, 58, 64-65, 82, 84, 99, 132, 136, 142-44, 146

Healing (*See* Autogenic Psycho-physical rehearsal)
Hill, Napoleon 42, 60, 82, 94
Hippocampus 32

I

Inappropriate forces (*See also* Appropriate forces) 25, 27, 29, 54-55, 96
Inhibiting forces 26
Insight 1, 7, 15, 17, 23, 45-46, 48, 71, 92, 94, 96, 100, 119, 128-29, 133, 139
Inspiration 97, 130, 133
Intercostal breathing (*See* Breathing, six levels of, mid-breathing)
Intuition 68, 119, 133

J

Jacob the Baker 130
Jensen, Bernard 81
"Jerusalem" 57
Jewish Meditation: A Practical Guide 12
Journal 20, 22-30, 36, 40, 49, 55-56, 62, 65, 86, 115-17, 138

K

Kaplan, Rabbi Aryeh 12

L

L Fields (*See also* Burr, Dr. Harold Saxton) 4-5
Langer, Ellen 81
Langley Porter Neuro-psychiatric Institute 35
Law of equivalent returns 46-48

Law of harmony (*See* Universal law of harmony)
Laws of thermodynamics 7-10, 66
Lewis, C.S. 95-96
Log Sheet for AAM 24

M

Maxwell, James Clerk 3, 123, 142
Meditation 1-3, 6, 9, 12, 19-27, 29-30, 40, 44-45, 48, 57, 59, 63, 65, 69, 78, 80-85, 90, 95-108, 111-21, 124-38, 140-42, 145-46, 154
   basic techniques 135-38
   breathing 137-38
   projecting your horizon 135-36
   relaxing 136-37
   reviewing 138
Meditation on objects 103-04
Menninger Clinic 35-36
Micro volts (*See also* Brain wave, Amplitude) 18, 41, 137
Milton, John 82
Mindfulness 81
"M.S. Notebooks" 141

N

Newton, Sir Isaac 8-9
Newton's Laws of Motion 8-9, 22-23
Non-attachment 68-76, 102, 125, 127, 135, 142

P

Paraconscious mind 13, 15-19, 21, 25-27, 29, 38, 40, 45-46, 48, 50-54, 56, 58-59, 62-63, 67-68, 70-71, 73-76,
81-83, 85, 87-88, 90-94, 99-107, 109-12, 117, 119, 121, 127, 133-35, 139-40, 144-45
Paradoxical breathing (*See* Breathing, six levels of, correct breathing)
Pelvic breathing (*See* Breathing, six levels of, full breathing)
Permanent Creative Principle 122-23
Pert, Candace 14
Pituitary gland 32
Popp, Dr. Fritz-Albert 5-6
"Proverbs of Hell" 121
Psycho-physical rehearsal 57-79, 98-99, 134-35, 137
   intent 74-76
   part one 44, 61, 77-78
   part two 45, 62-65, 78
   process 67-68
   reaction versus response 70-72
   spontaneity 76-78
   thought patterns 66-67

R

Regulating energy 5-6
Reich, Wilhelm 136
Renounce and enjoy 140
Repressed emotion 40-41
Ringer, Robert 81
RNA 5

S

Schwarz, Jack 2, 22, 35, 40, 77, 81, 106, 117, 155
Screwtape Letters, The 95
Sea of electromagnetic radiation 3-4
Spontaneity 42, 46, 68, 72, 76

States of consciousness (*See also* Alpha, Beta, Delta, and Theta) 31, 35, 41

Strauch, Ralph 81

Subconscious mind 13-19, 22, 25-27, 29, 33-34, 36-37, 41, 46-47, 50, 58-59, 63, 67-68, 70, 74, 82-84, 93-94, 99, 133-34, 139, 144-45

Symbolism 81, 91-92, 105, 108, 111-13, 115

T

Thalamus 32

Theta brain wave states 16-18, 36, 38-41, 49, 58, 90, 93, 102-03, 106, 108, 114-16, 127, 137

Theta breathing 38

Think and Grow Rich 82

Total mind 12-13, 18-21, 27, 42, 45, 48, 60, 70, 83-84, 100-01, 119, 129, 133

Transcendence 26-28, 43, 48, 54, 60, 63, 66, 70-71, 74, 79, 83-85, 87, 90, 92, 96, 103-04, 138-40

U

Universal law of harmony 9, 46-48, 58, 65, 142

Universal mind 1-3, 6-8, 10-19, 21-22, 26, 28-29, 43-46, 48, 51-52, 54, 56-63, 65-68, 71, 74-75, 77-81, 83, 88, 90-91, 93-94, 96, 98-99, 101-02, 105-06, 108-09, 111-12, 115, 118- 21, 124, 127-28, 130-31, 133-40, 144-46

GIVE THE GIFT OF PROSPERITY AND FULFILLMENT TO YOUR FRIENDS AND COLLEAGUES

ORDER FORM

YES, I want ___ copies of *Mind Map: Your Guide to Prosperity and Fulfillment* at $16.95 each, plus $3 shipping per book. (Ohio residents please include $1.19 state sales tax.) Canadian orders must be accompanied by a postal money order in U.S. funds. Allow 30 days for delivery.

___ Check/money order enclosed

Charge my ___ VISA ___ MasterCard

Name _____ Phone (__) _____

Organization _____

Address _____

City/State/Zip _____

Card # _____ Exp. Date _____

Signature _____

**Look in your leading bookstore or
Call your credit card orders to:**

1-800-950-4688

Make your check payable and return to:

Health Associates, Ltd.
P.O. Box 188009
University Heights, Ohio 44118